ROUTLEDGE LIBRARY EDITIONS:
THE NINETEENTH-CENTURY NOVEL

Volume 30

COURTSHIP AND THE ENGLISH NOVEL

COURTSHIP AND THE ENGLISH NOVEL

Feminist Readings in the Fiction of George Meredith

JANET HOROWITZ MURRAY

LONDON AND NEW YORK

First published in 1987 by Garland Publishing Inc.

This edition first published in 2016
by Routledge
4 Park Square, Milton Park, Abingdon, Oxon OX14 4RN
605 Third Avenue, New York, NY 10017

Routledge is an imprint of the Taylor & Francis Group, an informa business

© 1987 Janet Horowitz Murray

All rights reserved. No part of this book may be reprinted or reproduced or utilised in any form or by any electronic, mechanical, or other means, now known or hereafter invented, including photocopying and recording, or in any information storage or retrieval system, without permission in writing from the publishers.

Trademark notice: Product or corporate names may be trademarks or registered trademarks, and are used only for identification and explanation without intent to infringe.

British Library Cataloguing in Publication Data
A catalogue record for this book is available from the British Library

ISBN: 978-1-138-67777-7 (Set)
ISBN: 978-1-315-55928-5 (Set) (ebk)
ISBN: 978-1-138-67168-3 (Volume 30) (hbk)
ISBN: 978-1-138-67170-6 (Volume 30) (pbk)
ISBN: 978-1-315-61683-4 (Volume 30) (ebk)

Publisher's Note
The publisher has gone to great lengths to ensure the quality of this reprint but points out that some imperfections in the original copies may be apparent.

Disclaimer
The publisher has made every effort to trace copyright holders and would welcome correspondence from those they have been unable to trace.

COURTSHIP AND THE ENGLISH NOVEL

*Feminist Readings in the
Fiction of George Meredith*

JANET HOROWITZ MURRAY

*Garland Publishing, Inc.
New York & London
1987*

Copyright © 1987 by Janet Horowitz Murray
All Rights Reserved

Library of Congress Cataloging-in-Publication Data

Murray, Janet Horowitz, 1946–
Courtship and the English novel.

(Harvard dissertations in American and English literature)
Thesis (Ph. D.) — Harvard University, 1974.
Bibliography: p.
1. Meredith, George, 1828–1909 — Criticism and interpretation. 2. Courtship in literature.
3. Feminism and literature. I. Title. II. Series.
PR5014.M87 1987   823'.8   87-15009
ISBN 0-8240-0068-4

The volumes in this series are printed on acid-free, 250-year-life paper.

Printed in the United States of America

Courtship and the English Novel:
Feminist Readings in the Fiction of George Meredith

A thesis presented

by

Janet Ruth Horowitz

to

The Department of English and
American Literature and Language

in partial fulfillment of the
requirement for the degree of

Doctor of Philosophy

in the subject of

English and American
Literature and Language

Harvard University
Cambridge, Massachusetts

January, 1974

CONTENTS

Introduction: Courtship and the English Novel 1

Chapter I: <u>The Ordeal of Richard Feverel</u>:
    A Novel with a Hero 39

Chapter II: The Egoist and the New Woman 83

Chapter III: <u>Diana of the Crossways</u>: The
    Heroine of Reality 121

Bibliography 173
    Works by George Meredith
    Other Works

INTRODUCTION

Courtship and the English Novel

The essays which follow deal with the three major novels of George Meredith. I will be addressing two questions which are ultimately related. These questions are, first, in what ways do Meredith's novels deviate from the conventional narrative patterns of English fiction? and, second, how does Meredith's feminism affect his writing? I will be arguing that the unconventionality of Meredith's novels reflects the unconventionality of his vision of social relationships.

Meredith is an unpopular novelist partly because of his idiosyncratic and often opaque style, which I will be discussing in the last section of this Introduction. But he is also difficult to read because his novels cheat our expectations in broader ways. For example, the reader is confused to find a marriage in the middle instead of at the end of the novel, or an important discovery coming when all seems resolved, or characters one expects to be rewarded dying quite suddenly. Meredith's novels are full of such jarring events which surprise us not because they are unlike life, but because they are unlike other novels. My essays are centered on this problem--on the disconcerting apparent disregard for continuity and symmetry in Meredith's writing.

In each essay I have further attempted to demonstrate how the novel embodies Meredith's very modern views of the relations between the sexes. My reading of <u>The Ordeal of Richard Feverel</u>, <u>The Egoist</u>, and <u>Diana of the Crossways</u> takes Meredith's feminism seriously as part of the substance of his imagination, and I have pressed these novels, sorted through their configurations of character and event, in order to discover how life appears to a feminist imagination of the late nineteenth century. These essays have separate though related areas of concern. In discussing <u>Richard Feverel</u>, one of the most maligned and yet one of the most ambitious novels of the century, I have tried to uncover the associations implicit in Meredith's creation of male and female characters, and I have attempted to articulate what I see as a very clear effort on his part to rearrange the English novel's stereotypical notions of masculinity and femininity. In discussing <u>The Egoist</u> I have largely avoided the very widely discussed characterization of what we now call "male chauvinism" in the creation of Willoughby Patterne himself. Instead, I have looked closely at Meredith's exhilarating imaginative grasp of the inward costs of Clara's imprisonment. In the third essay I have tried to make clear the subtlety of <u>Diana of the Crossways</u> in presenting a woman living on the very edge of what is permissible or even comprehensible to her society.

In his way, Meredith is a great breaker of taboos. He is always trying to give substance to emotional tensions and social complexities for which he has little language and precedents which are more confusing than helpful. George Meredith was not a first-rate novelist. He was not a Richardson or a Lawrence; he had not the talent to invent a new form or to reinvent a broken genre. Yet at his best he had an alertness of the first order, and so even when his novels fail, they fail in interesting ways. In fact if his novels were more conventionally pleasing, they would probably be far less rewarding. The things he cared most to grapple with were things that he could not quite control well enough to make his readers comfortable. The Egoist, his most popular, most finished novel was very disappointing to Meredith himself, and felt to him as if he were writing a lie.[1]

Meredith's very difficulties in constructing his novels, the resistance he met in trying to embody in an English novel the world he saw and ached to give expression to, are tremendously revealing of the ways in which more successful novels shape human experience. In trying to tell new truths

---

[1] Although readers most often complain about Meredith's style rather than his plots, it is quite clear that bad stylists such as Defoe, Fenimore Cooper, Dreiser, and Hardy are widely read despite their confusing narrative voices. I think this is because the reader never loses faith in the logic of the plot. In a narrative form, I have a strong disposition to believe that a construable story is more important than a lucid style.

Meredith is always right on target in what he destroys, always penetrating in pointing to what is comfortable fantasy in other novels. Meredith's heroines may not always be convincing, but after meeting them one knows better what to think of Amelia Sedley and Becky Sharpe, and Esther Summerson and Ada Clare.

In the pages which follow I will have much to say about Meredith's rupturing of traditional values and literary conventions. In this introduction I would like to make clear what I mean by those conventions, and more importantly I would like to put Meredith's effort in perspective by examining the imaginative vision of other, greater English novelists with particular regard to their notions of sex, love, and marriage. I will discuss two pairs of novelists: Richardson and Fielding, and Austen and Charlotte Bronte. Each pair represents in miniature two polarities of English fiction. Richardson and Austen belong to the strain which depicts the struggle of the individual against self and towards integration in the social order. I am associating this strain with the epistolary tradition. Fielding and Bronte write largely from the opposite impulse, which is related to the picaresque tradition in which the individual struggles to affirm self against a hostile society. Novels of the first sort tend to be psychological and those of the second sociological in orientation. I mean these classifications to be heuristic and suggestive rather than restrictive and rigid. The importance of these polarities to an understanding of Meredith is that they constituted alternatives from which he had to choose the direction of his own fiction. The burden of these essays will be to explore the ways in which he worked within and against the conventions of each of these major traditions of the English novel.

-2-

Samuel Richardson and Henry Fielding in an odd collaboration of mutual antagonism together invented the English novel. One can imagine their creation of the genre as a double birth of a sister and a brother--Richardson's <u>Pamela</u> and Fielding's "sequel" <u>Joseph Andrews</u>. For these two novels, taken together with their extensions, <u>Clarissa</u> and <u>Tom Jones</u>, suggest the direction of the next two centuries of fiction-writing in England, and to a lesser extent in Europe and America as well.

Significantly, as the titles indicate, each of these prototypical novels tells the life story of one person. Ian Watt[2] has lucidly detailed the newness of such specificity in subject matter and the appropriateness of such detailed and specific stories to the new middle-class post-

---

[2] in <u>The Rise of the Novel</u> (Berkeley, 1967).

puritan reading public interested in the primacy of the individual as a spiritual and economic unit.[3] He has also documented the new importance of marriage choices in the early eighteenth century and its bearing upon Richardson's brilliant innovation of the single courtship as a unifying device. The association of the individual life-story (used by Defoe) with the focus on sex and courtship (known to Defoe only as a money relation) marked the birth of the novel.

It is worth thinking about what this focus on the individual and his or her marriage choice includes. One very important novelty in the novel's treatment of courtship is the pattern of a moral education leading to marriage that is established by Richardson and Fielding and recurs in the plots of those who follow them. As Watt has described, the eighteenth century marked the breakdown of the individual's identification with larger social units, and the establishment of the conjugal family as the primary unit of social organization. The novel helped to articulate and indeed to create the new mythos for this new social organization. As marriage became the central social arrangement, really the building block of the larger society, the education leading

---

[3] See especially Chapters I, II, III, V, and VI.

[4] Ibid., Chapter V.

to marriage took on the importance of an initiation rite into the society at large. The novel both described this educative process and performed it for its readers. In Watt's words: "One of the main functions of the novel since Richardson, it may be suggested, has been to serve as a fictional initiation rite into the most fundamental mystery of its society"--the mystery of sex and marriage.[5]

When Mr. B. stops trying to rape his servant Pamela and decides to propose marriage it is because he has undergone an education at her hands. His decision to get married reflects his changed notions of class and virtue. Similarly, Pamela herself learns a new social decorum from her husband in the much-lamented long second section of the novel. The lovers initiate one another into proper social conduct and receive one another as the reward of their changed behavior. Richardson is educating his readers as well. He is clearly, consciously writing a conduct book as well as a novel. He is instructing his audience in the right way to behave with regard to the suddenly very difficult and confusing social institution of marriage. And he is also setting up a continuing pattern in the English novel of a moral education preparing the protagonist to make the proper marriage choice

---

[5] Ibid., p. 174. In this connection, see Dr. Johnson's Rambler No. 4 in which he described the educative role of the novel for the young.

or to deserve the proper spouse.[6]

    This pattern is quite central to the plot of Tom Jones. Tom is set to learning "prudence"--that most socializing virtue--in order to be worthy of Sophia. Of course the emotional tone of the novel is completely opposed to prudence and associates it with the calculating Blifil. Yet Fielding sets his picaro running through his thousand pages of adventure, obstensibly to teach him prudence, to make him worthy of integration into the larger community. The novel ends with the assurance that "there is not a neighbor, a tenant or a servant, who doth not most gracefully bless the day when Mr. Jones was married to his Sophia." Tom's mishaps prepare him for marriage to Sophia, an event which makes the entire community happy and whole. The courtship is the framing story and the significance is clearly social. Characters as diverse as Emma Woodhouse and Edward Waverly recapitulate this story of moral education within a highly societal context leading to a proper marriage choice which benefits the community at large.[7] It is important to remem-

---

    [6]Pamela's moral education is limited to the defense of her virginity, since that negative virtue had become the highest value in the moral life of women. Her predicament is none the less educational in that it tests her mettle. She passes the test and receives as a reward the man she has so honorably rejected. This renunciation pattern is central to the English novel's approach to moral dilemmas as I discuss in Chapter II.

    [7]From the eighteenth to the nineteenth century novel the

ber the highly communal nature of the virtues in *Pamela* and *Tom Jones* since they prove typical of the objects of moral education in English fiction in general.

Coming back to the double paternity of Richardson and Fielding, there lies behind them the separate traditions of two kinds of prose fiction: the one epistolary, the other picaresque. These two impulses are related responses to the eighteenth century perception of an increasingly privatized and disconnected world. It is of course always useful to remember that Richardson wrote a book of model letters which also served as models of difficult relations. The germ of *Pamela* itself is found in one of these letters which is to be written by low-born parents to their servant daughter whose virtue is endangered by her master.[8] The fact that there was a demand for such models is testimony to the confusion and discontinuity of social relations among the

---

community which is benefitted by a marriage tends to narrow from the old feudal dependents of a country landlord like Tom Jones or Mr. Knightley to a close domestic circle which includes friends and dependents such as we often have at the end of a novel by Dickens. In the twentieth century the people who are benefitted by the marriage at the end of a novel are usually a fantasized posterity such as Birkin or Mellors imagine, although more frequently there is no marriage at all.

[8] See Samuel Richardson, *Familiar Letters on the most Important Occasions in Common Life* (1741), letters CXXXVIII and CXXIX, "A Father to a Daughter in Service, on hearing of her Master's attempting her Virtue," and "The Daughter's Answer."

newly formed puritan middle class reading public.[9] And the letter form itself is significant of the Richardsonian strategy for facing the privatized, discontinuous world, for a letter is both a solitary delving into one's own consciousness and a rope thrown out to the outside world, seeking connectedness. Certainly the letters from Richardson's isolated heroines are especially significant of this separateness, of this attempt to discover what is proper and improper, and of this search for social ties. The novel begins with this exploration of the tension between the individual and his or her passions and the demands of the society for certain decorums and proprieties of feeling as well as of behavior.

The picaresque comes at the problem from the other side. The picaro has no significant relation to himself and characteristically does not question his own desires or behavior. He is usually too busy staying alive in a world whose discontinuity is emblemized by violence, unpredictable hostility, constant assault and deprivation. This world is certainly the imaginative reverse of the social vision which asks the individual to change in order to be accepted into society. Pamela's defense of her virginity is a way of staying connected with her world. Joseph Andrew's preser-

---

[9]Think of the helplessness behind any letter to "Dear Abby." The question her correspondents are always posing is "How do I keep the social fabric together? Where do I draw the line of acceptable and unacceptable behavior?"

vation of his virginity starts out as a parody of Pamela's but it becomes an emblem of his relation to his world. Like Lazarillo de Tormes, the prototypical picaro, Joseph is beaten and tricked by everyone he meets. Violation is the pattern of social conduct; therefore embattled defense of virginity is an emblematic stance. Although Joseph does end up married and wealthy like his sister, he does not set up a household which like hers is a blessing to the neighborhood. Instead, he retires into complete isolation (his parents have made an Augustan retreat; Joseph and his bride go off to some place more remote than the Andrews' virtual hermitage). He walls himself off from a society too corrupt for him to assimilate into it. His education teaches him no skills; his character remains static. He takes his unviolated innocence and barricades it from the rest of society. Such is Fielding's parodic vision of Pamela.

Significantly enough, Fielding wrote in the "Preface" to Joseph Andrews, a document of considerable importance since it is a serious attempt to define the new genre, that the proper target for the Comic Novel is Affectation, that is, the pretence of being what one is not or of hiding what one is. Fielding saw Pamela's chastity as affectation and he parodied it twice: in Shamela, as an artifice for marry- above her station, and in Joseph Andrews, as prudishness. But if Richardson makes Pamela ambiguous and exaggerated enough to provoke such ridicule, Clarissa makes clear how seriously he took Pamela's fight against Mr. B.

In fact it is quite clear that chastity was economically essential to women in the eighteenth century, as it had never been before.[10] And Fielding was well aware of that. But no doubt Pamela and Clarissa both must have seemed affected and ridiculous to him as practitioners of the code of decorum and delicacy which is their chief protection against loss of social station. Affectation for Fielding meant covering up who you really are, what you really want. But of course, as Ian Watt points out, the new sexual code of the early eighteenth century, which denies women the freedom to acknowledge sexual feelings for a suiter until after marriage,[11] sets up the situation Richardson works from.[12] Mr. B. and Pamela, Lovelace and Clarissa, are engaged in an elaborate battle in

---

[10] See Christopher Hill, "Clarissa Harlowe and Her Times," Puritanism and Revolution: The English Revolution of the Seventeenth Century (New York: Schocken, 1958), Part II, Chapter 14. Hill also makes an interesting connection between the rise of the custom of property marriage among the middle class and the emergence of "sex-war" such as Richardson describes, and such as had been depicted in the Restoration Drama. In Chapter II, I will be talking about the connection between this restoration mode and the novels of Richardson, Austen, and Meredith.

[11] Fielding was certainly well aware of the exigencies of the new social arrangement. He parodies them in Lady Booby's disconcerting boast that she had loved her husband passionately but had had the modesty to make sure he never suspected it, Joseph Andrews, Book IV, Chapter VI.

[12] Watt, pp. 167-9.

which the mention of stockings, the manner of phrasing a proposal, the position of a tea-cup are all significant strategical advances. The system of Restoration sparring is indeed affected since the real aims of the lovers cannot be mentioned. Watt describes Pamela as "a sermon and a striptease"[13] and indeed it is this constant tension between unmentionable desires and social euphemisms (which ends by attaching sexual meaning to everything), which makes <u>Pamela</u> and <u>Clarissa</u> so effective on both levels.

Richardson's novels are about the development of a certain kind of affectation which Richardson called decorum or delicacy; an affectation which allowed women to live in a world which is always threatening violation. Pamela and Clarissa confront a reality much like that which Joseph Andrews discovers and their response to this constant threat of violence is a kind of game-playing, a manipulation of word and gesture which protects them from certain kinds of violation, although it cannot ultimately defend them. Like Millamant (whom I am sure Fielding would have found affected), Richardson's heroines have only their quick tongues to keep them safe. Pamela is a "sauce-box" and Clarissa is an actress because they are on guard against violation every time they see their lovers. Their only defense is a kind of insult and the elaboration of a social persona which acts as

---

[13] Watt, p. 173.

a barricade. They are constantly fighting off the symbolic violations of improper words and gestures because they are ultimately powerless to fight off an actual rape. They build their line of defense off in front of them as an indeed affected persona, so that they can fight the battle on terms that they have some control over. Once the social barriers are crossed and the social personas destroyed there is nothing standing between them and the complete social "ruin" of sexual violation.

Paradoxically the false social facade is infinitely more revealing of personality and character than a less mannered persona. We know much more of how Clarissa and Lovelace think and feel than we know of Tom Jones. In opposing affectation, Fielding is also opposing a sort of complexity of character (in the moral sense) which goes along with complexity of characterization. He cannot deal with an ambivalent Pamela--he prefers a hypocritical Shamela, whom he can understand and laugh at; and indeed he tends to admire only simple-minded forms of goodness--the innocence of a Parson Adams, the "natural goodness of heart" of a Tom Jones.[14] Because Fielding has no tolerance for a mixed

---

[14] This simplistic moral stance, which is characteristic of the Victorian novel, is especially apparent and especially Victorian in Fielding's unsuccessful and terribly pessimistic novel, *Amelia*. The sentimentalism of the novel is a shock after *Tom Jones*, and the simpering, long-suffering domestic heroine could very well have given her name to Thackeray's Amelia Sedley.

motive he is blind to the psychological complexity that is Richardson's forte.

Richardson presents the solution to the problem of the social demands made upon passion which is most favored by English novelists: adjustment by the elaboration of a social persona. Another word for this persona could be character. English novels are always concerned with the formation of character and they characterize generally by the detailed examination of individual conscience, especially as the conscience functions to adapt the individual will to the social good. Tom Jones's supposed lesson in prudence echoes this pattern and shows how deeply the presumption of the necessity to adjust to the society is imbedded in the English spirit. For even Fielding, who does not really believe in it at all, tries to subscribe to the possibility of an accommodation between the individual and his society in this, his most optimistic novel. More than any other literature, English fiction is deeply commited to the Richardsonian view that self-examination and the development of individual conscience, especially in the context of social relations and sexuality, should lead to the development of a moral social persona. After Fielding it is hard to find an important hero of English fiction whose desires are not open to question and in need of chastening before the happy marriage can be achieved. In the English novel, obstacles to happiness are almost always presented as internal, never within the scope of the society itself. In the American and French novel the price of civilization is always open to question. But in English fiction the primary question is always how the individual will adjust to the rules of the game and get married.

Both Tom Jones and Clarissa are up against external enemies and internal weaknesses. But for Tom the major problem is circumventing his enemies out there on the high road; while for Clarissa, imprisoned within a set of rooms, the major problem is determining over and over again her own moral stance. It is of course significant that the stories of adaptation should begin with women, and that their brother novels, so to speak, should be so much less concerned with self-questioning and so much more concerned with grabbing what one wants. Though the female model becomes the more important prototype, Tom Jones makes clear what the choices were for novelists faced with the questions of the contending claims of the individual and the society. For the overwhelming majority of English novelists affectation rather than action became the solution.

-3-

Pamela preserves her virginity and achieves wealth and marriage (the objectionable subtitle of the novel is "Virtue

Rewarded"); Clarissa gets raped and dies. Mary Wollstonecraft, writing one of the first tracts for sexual equality at the end of the century, remarks of Richardson that he "must have had strange notions of honour and virtue [to write of Clarissa's being "robbed or her honour"]. For miserable, beyond all names of misery is the condition of a being who could be degraded without its own consent."[15] But of course within the context of the novel the rape does indeed degrade Clarissa, in the sense of lowering her social standing, and it does touch her directly, if unjustly, changing who she is to herself and to her society. It is interesting that she is not merely overpowered by Lovelace, she is raped while drugged. She is not merely innocent of volition in the act which is her fall, she is completely ignorant of it. Yet she is, within the logic of the plot, internally changed just the same. Her character is such that the degradation of this act which she can hardly be said to have experienced leads her straight to her death.

The very ambiguity of Clarissa's social position is partially responsible for her death. She is neither maid nor wife, debauchee nor virgin. She cannot go to a nunnery as a French heroine would. There is simply no place for her in her society. Clarissa is the first of a long series of

---

[15] *A Vindication of the Rights of Woman* (1792) Chapter IV.

heroines, most of them dating from the late nineteenth century, who die at the end of novels largely because they have slipped out of the social scheme, overstepped cultural boundaries, and their creators don't know what to do with them. They have experienced too much to be assimilated back into their society. In a reversal of an initiation ritual, they go off into the world and learn too much to come home. Maggie Tulliver, Hardy's Tess, Lily Bart (in The House of Mirth), Rachel Vinrace (in Woolf's The Voyage Out) are just a few examples of the many heroines who cannot survive once they have gone beyond the limit of what is construable by their culture. In killing off Clarissa, Richardson is saying that there is no place in his marriage-centered society for a woman who has been raped. Like the recent terrible example of the Bengali women raped by Pakistani soldiers, in a culture in which women are property, those whose ownership is disputable have no place. The things which happen to a woman, where women are marketable goods, are more significant than the things which happen within her.

The rape of Clarissa is only one one of many such violations. Dorothy Van Ghent[16] and David Daiches[17] are among

---

[16] in "On Clarissa Harlow" in The English Novel: form and function (New York: Harper Torchbooks, 1961), p. 62.

[17] in "Samuel Richardson" in Literary Essays (Edinburgh and London: Oliver and Boyd, Ltd., 1966), pp. 26-42, reprinted

those who have pointed out the surprising absence of sensuality in Richardson's novels. Instead of sensual pleasure there is an elaboration of the archetypes of femininity and masculinity, chiefly around the concepts of the power relations which became exaggerated in the eighteenth century. Here is Van Ghent's excellent description of "the Clarissa-symbol," as she calls it:

> [T]he erotic situations that are dramatized are excessively simple and abstract, limited to suggestions of bodily violence or violence done to clothes (stabbing or tearing) and the converse, suggestions of violence suffered (weeping, fainting, dying). Clarissa herself is offered as the ideal woman in her purity and debility--and these qualities, too, are extraordinarily limited abstractions from the complex qualities that might be conceived as making up complete womanhood; at the same time, pure and debile as she is, paradoxically she offers an ideal of the sexual woman (in the world of this book), the physically desirable woman.

In an age which denied woman sexual desire, the image of sexuality in woman is not the truly sexual woman, but the sexually desirable woman, the commodity to be enjoyed. And the enjoyment is necessarily a violation. Van Ghent continues:

> She is a kind of love goddess, a Venus, she is not the Venus of the Renaissance, with an erotic apparatus of Mayflowers, delicately tinted veils, sinuous tresses, zephyrs, lutes, and cupids, suggesting many enjoyments for the senses, suggesting also the aesthetic act of contemplation. She is much more abstract than that. She is the love goddess of the

---

in *Twentieth Century Interpretations of "Pamela"* (New Jersey, 1969), pp. 14-25. The discussion referred to appears on p. 25.

> Puritan middle class of the English eighteenth century, of the bourgeois family, and of mercantile society. She is pure (to be paraded for the sight as an expensive chattel--or, in later generations, to show herself voluntarily as "career girl"), and yet to be violated (for in a society that has desexualized its professed mores, sex is a violation), but still to be seen while she is being violated (for sex insists on perpetuating its attractions, but they must be enjoyed by proxy, as in the movies, or *sub rosa*).[18]

It is of vital importance to an understanding of the English novel, and of cultural attitudes toward sexuality still powerfully alive, to realize that these novels which first celebrated marriage as we know it also celebrated rape. There is hardly a novel written in the century which we still read today in which rape or the threat of rape does not play an important part. And of course the eighteenth century subgenre, the Gothic novel, is entirely concerned with the obsessional repetition of the threatened violation of the virgin.

The image of masculinity which complements the debilitated, vulnerable woman is summed up with equal strength in Van Ghent's article:

> Somewhere Joseph Conrad speaks of "the fascination of the abomination," a phrase which applies nicely to the image of "the man" in Clarissa; for as the image grows by reiteration and variation into a symbol, attractive elements are fused with the repellent elements, so that the abominable toadlike reptilian "man" becomes demonically fascinating: a creature obsessed with the desire to violate virginal, high-

---

[18] Van Ghent, p. 50.

> minded, helpless womanhood, and so single-tracked in
> his passion to destroy this divinity that he, too,
> assumes divine stature; he is the evil divinity,
> the devil himself.[19]

Clarissa is only the violent version which makes clear the emotional forces which are present but slightly more subdued in the nuptual hymn of Pamela. Watt speaks of the courtship in Pamela as initiating the same new formulation of sexual roles, marking "a very notable epiphany in the history of our culture: the emergence of a new, fully developed and immensely influential stereotype of the feminine role" which has been "an essential feature of our civilization over the past two hundred years" and "embodies a more complete and comprehensive separation between the male and female roles than had previously existed."[20]

To think of the hearty sexuality of Shakespeare's women is to see how far women had come in being desexualized in the course of a century. Puritanism was largely responsible for the new sexual ethic which insisted upon feminine chastity. At the same time women lost a great deal of their economic power and most of their usefulness as co-workers with men, as the household trades were replaced by manufacturing.[21] Early industrial capitalism had no place for

---

[19] Ibid., p. 51.

[20] Watt, pp. 161-2.

[21] For the drastic change in women's economic circumstances,

female labor outside the factory, and the idleness of middle-class wives came to be valued as a sign of wealth. By the end of the century Mary Wollstonecraft was complaining bitterly that the women she saw around her behaved as if they had no souls, and were put on earth to be ornamental and physically handicapped. It is pathetic to read today her passionate cries for exercise and fresh air for middle-class girls. Although prostitution flourished, and factories offered equality of exploitation along with men, for women who wished to live comfortably, marriage was certainly as Charlotte Lucas thought it, "the only honourable provision for well-educated young women of small fortune, and however uncertain of giving happiness . . . their pleasantest preservation from want."[22]

For such a society, Pamela became the model fictional representative of womanhood. Utter and Needham[23] have traced the careers of "Pamela's Daughters," vapid girls whose appeal lies in their pastoral innocence and vulnerability to attack. The heroines of the Gothic novel and the real

---

see Alice Clark, Working Life of Women in the Seventeenth Century (New York: Dutton, 1919); Frederick W. Tickner, Women in English Economic History (London, 1923); I.B. O'Malley, Women in Subjection (London: Camelot, 1933).

[22] Jane Austen, Pride and Prejudice, Volume I, Chapter xxii.

[23] R.P. Utter and G.B. Needham, Pamela's Daughters (New York: Macmillan, 1936).

and imagined victims of De Sade also owe their trials to Richardson in part. And we must not forget that today some variation of Fay Wray in the hairy clutches of King Kong is still a powerful erotic image in our culture.

The novel form certainly begins with this image of male/female relations, and the relative absence of sexuality in the works of Dickens and Thackeray comes partly from an unwillingness to deal with the violence of this conventional pattern. On the other hand, the Victorian novel repeats the pattern without the overt sexual component. In Dickens and Thackeray we see defined our very modern conception of the world as one divided into two parts: the corrupt male world of business and exploitation, and the innocent passive helpless feminine world of human affection centered around the conjugal home. The opposed moral worlds of one's job at IBM and one's home in Westchester, now a familiar reality of modern life[24] emerges in the Victorian novel as the middle-

---

[24] An engaging recent public example of our acceptance of this concept of separate spheres is former Presidential attorney Kalmbach's testimony in the Watergate investigation that he looked into John Erhlichman's eyes and reminded him that he had met Mrs. Kalmbach before accepting at Erhlichman's urging the responsibility of raising and delivering pay-off money for the Watergate burglars. Erhlichman denied the charge but affirmed the solemnity of such an appeal if it had been made. No one on the Senate Subcommittee asked Erhlichman why his relationship with Kalmbach as a husband should be upon a higher moral plane than that of the White House.

class formulation of sexual roles is extended into two opposing spheres of being where completely conflicting morality obtains. Again the guiding impulse is power. To be effective, whether one is male or female, becomes suspect. The purest moral position is (to use an image Meredith was fond of) beneath someone else's chariot wheels.

In Chapters I and II, I will be discussing Meredith's very unusual response to this convention of Victorian thinking and Victorian fiction. But it is enough for the present to point out the continuum between the sex role typing of the eighteenth century novel and the notions of good and evil of the Victorian novel, a continuum which thousands of scenes of imperilled innocence from <u>Pamela</u> onward helped to shape as a collective imaginative vision of the moral life.

-4-

Jane Austen, the first major woman writer in the English language, began her career with a parody of a Gothic novel. Like Fielding she had a primarily comic imagination which was spurred on by the absurdities of others. The improbabilities of the Gothic conventions provided the impetus to her imagination which Pamela's prudishness provided to Fielding's. Interestingly enough <u>Northanger Abbey</u> does not parody the ferocity of the Gothic villain nor the debility of the

Gothic heroine.[25] Catherine's gullibility as a novel-reader, the inappropriateness of her expectations to the quiet English world around her, and the rudeness and foolishness of her intrusion of expectations of adventure on the civilized world around her form the chief comic targets of the novel. The castigation of Catherine, which turns her into a sensible young lady, is a highly derivative effort going back to Eliza Heywood and Fanny Burney. Heywood's <u>Betsey Thoughtless</u> and Burney's <u>Evelina</u>, for example, concern green and gullible young girls who go through narrow scrapes usually involving the threat of sexual violation, and learn to be more ladylike and sensible. Then they get married.

Jane Austen basically builds upon this pattern. From Catherine to Ann Eliot, the heroine of <u>Persuasion</u>, her last novel, Austen draws women who must learn to be more realistic, more sensible, more ladylike, and who are rewarded for this moral education with marriage.[26] And the virtues which they

---

[25] The only time Austen takes notice of the excesses of the male Gothic spirit is in the character of Benwick in <u>Persuasion</u>, an admirer of Byron who is presented as a silly soppy adolescent. She never directly parodies the debility of the Gothic heroine, or creates a character like Beatrice in <u>Much Ado About Nothing</u> who by her wit and presence makes the conventional sterotypical woman (represented by Hero in the play) absurd. Elinor, in <u>Sense and Sensibility</u>, and Elizabeth, in <u>Pride and Prejudice</u>, act somewhat like Beatrice, but it is interesting to me that this very available comic strategy is not the one that occurs to Austen in writing her parody of the Gothic form, especially since she chooses instead to make the heroine's foolish rowdiness the comic target.

[26] It is worth noting that, following the tradition estab-

learn are primarily those of adaptation to the severe limits of their world. Jane Austen never questions the fundamental assumptions of her society. She shared with Mary Wollstonecraft a Johnsonian moral strenuousness braced with common sense and a scorn for the coddled, sheltered women who shudder at Elizabeth Bennet taking a walk alone. But Wollstonecraft sees that there is a whole social system behind such behavior. Jane Austen is deeply conservative. She hates poor foolish sixteen-year-old Lydia Bennet for running off with Wickham with disconcerting intensity, yet she has no indignation for the entailment of the Bennet estate away from the female line.[27]

Persuasion is the novel in which the world opens the most for her heroine. Virginia Woolf has movingly expressed the pathos of Austen's dying so soon after making such a move outward into the incorporation of new experience, as this novel so clearly signals.[28] Certainly it is the only

---

lished by Richardson, all her heroines marry up on the economic ladder, except Ann who lives in a much more troubled and realistic world than the other women, and who is going to make her home at sea rather than in the English home counties.

[27] Mrs. Bennet's frequent lamentations of her precarious future are signs of her weak character. The logic of the novel tells us that it is only sane and sensible to accept the entailment without quarrel. Elizabeth, for example, never has a moment's thought of how hard it will be to be some day forced to leave her only home.

[28] in "Jane Austen" in *The Common Reader: First Series*.

novel in which the heroine's lover is not at all her moral guide. The pattern which Heywood and Burney used of introducing an older male tutor for their ingenue heroines was modified by Austen considerably so that her heroines always learn not so much from their lovers as from the experience of loving. And in *Persuasion* this is more the case than ever before. However worthy Wentworth may be, the fact that he "went" is far more important than his "worth."[29] In other words, *Persuasion* is about adjusting to loneliness. It is about solitude and isolation--an isolation much more intense than Clarissa's imprisonment, for Ann Eliot must learn how to live with no significant relations to sustain her. But of course the reward of such moral growth is marriage to Wentworth.

Prison is a good image for the situation of women in general, and certainly for the heroines of British fiction. What else is Lowood School for Jane Eyre, the Grange for Catherine Earnshaw, Lowick Manor for Dorothea Brooke? But Jane Austen is the woman novelist most interested in making do within that prison. She virtually sings hymns to adjustment. Consider this famous description of Emma's life:

> Harriet, tempted by everything and swayed by half a word, was always very long at a purchase; and while she was still hanging over muslins and changing her mind, Emma went to the door for amusement.--Much

---

[29] The same is true of the worthy but absent Austin Wentworth in *The Ordeal of Richard Feverel*.

> could not be hoped from the traffic of even the
> busiest part of Highbury;--Mr. Perry walking hastily
> by, Mr. William Cox letting himself in at the office
> door, Mr. Cole's carriage horses returning from ex-
> ercise, or a stray letter-boy on an obstinate mule,
> were the liveliest objects she could presume to ex-
> pect; and when her eyes fell only on the butcher
> with his tray, a tidy old woman traveling homewards
> from shop with her full basket, two curs quarreling
> over a dirty bone, and a string of dawdling children
> round the baker's little bow-window eyeing the gin-
> gerbread, she knew she had no reason to complain,
> and was amused enough; quite enough still to stand
> at the door. A mind lively and at ease can do with
> seeing nothing, and can see nothing that does not
> answer.[30]

Emma has "no reason to complain" because she has no reason to expect more of the little town she lives in. She certainly has plenty of reason to complain of living in Highbury in the first place. It is not until the writing of _Persuasion_, however, that Austen confronts the loneliness of a life of Mr. William Cox, Mr. Cole, some fighting curs, a few children, and a tidy old woman. The answer to Emma's very real predicament of having nothing to occupy her and no one but Mrs. Weston and Mr. Knightley to converse profitably with for her entire life is the cultivation of a sunny temperament and a well-regulated mind. She learns to curb her disposition, to refrain from matchmaking and from teasing foolish Miss Bates, both quite understandable vices when you think about the confinement of her situation. Though Emma's character makes perfect sense within the context of the novel, if one steps

---

[30] _Emma_, Volume II, Chapter 9.

two paces back from it one finds oneself wondering how she restrains herself from poisoning her father, let alone insulting Mrs. Bates. But while we are reading the novel Emma's socialization seems perfectly reasonable and it is described with so much human complexity that it seems to rise above the level of mere acquiescence in imprisonment. Yet for all its real generosity and authority, this is a novel about the only intelligent and lively young woman in a country town, and it is important for the reader to acknowledge Austen's conscious choice of a structure which chastizes the girl for restlessness, vanity, and lack of restraint.

Compare the above quotation to this very similar description, written in Yorkshire some 40 years later. This is Jane Eyre's response to the peacefulness of Thornfield before the arrival of Mr. Rochester:

> Anybody may blame me who likes, when I add further that, now and then, when I took a walk by myself in the grounds; when I went down to the gates and looked through them along the road; or when, while Adele played with her nurse, and Mrs. Fairfax made jellies in the store-room, I climbed the three staircases, raised the trap-door of the attic, and having reached the leads, looked out afar over sequestered field and hill, and along the dim skyline--that then I longed for power of vision which might over-pass that limit; which might reach the busy world, towns, regions full of life I had heard of but never seen; that then I desired more of practical experience than I possessed; more of intercourse with my kind, of acquaintance with variety of character, than was here within my reach. I valued what was good in Mrs. Fairfax and what was good in Adele; but I believed in the existence of other and

> more vivid kinds of goodness, and what I believed
> in I wished to behold.[31]

Jane's final appeal to appropriate levels of valuation is oddly Austen-like. Mr. Cox and two fighting curs are certainly entertaining in their way, but what are we to expect of the lively mind not at ease with only such simple characters? Jane Eyre goes on to invoke the imagination as the refuge of the unsatisfied spirit, as Jane Austen had invoked the lively intellect. But the difference is that the comic sense does not seek for more passionate involvement in life, as the imaginative vision does. Jane wants to go out on the highroad and change the world to suit her expectations. Emma is content to change her expectations to suit the world. Jane's meditations here turn to almost a direct answer to Austen's description of Emma's situation:

> It is vain to say human beings ought to be satisfied
> with tranquility; they must have action; and they
> will make it if they cannot find it. Millions are
> condemned to a stiller doom than mine, and millions
> are in silent revolt against their lot. Nobody
> knows how many rebellions besides political rebel-
> lions ferment in the masses of life which people
> earth. Women are supposed to be very calm generally;
> but women feel just as men feel; they need exercise
> for their faculties, and a field for their efforts
> as much as their brothers do; they suffer from too
> rigid a constraint, too absolute a stagnation, pre-
> cisely as men would suffer; and it is narrow-minded
> in their more privileged fellow-creatures to say that
> they ought to confine themselves to making puddings
> and knitting stockings, to playing on the piano and
> embroidering bags. It is thoughtless to condemn them,

---

[31] *Jane Eyre*, Chapter XII.

> or laugh at them, if they seek to do more or learn more than custom has pronounced necessary for their sex.[32]

The difference between Austen and Bronte is similar to that between Richardson and Fielding. Jane Eyre is a picaro, one who questions her society rather than her own emotional necessities. Her enemy is external rather than internal. Emma discovers that her battle with the dullness of the outside world is a failure and adjusts herself to her circumstances. The conflict between passion and adjustment is exactly what the novel has always been about, and Austen and the Brontes represent strikingly contrasting stances in that dilemma.[33]

But the mainstream of the English novel is clearly with Austen in celebrating adjustment to the confinement imposed upon the individual by the society. It seems to me quite

---

[32] In Chapter 4 of *A Room of One's Own*, Virgina Woolf cites this passage as the sudden intrusion of Charlotte Bronte's own voice, and she finds the reference to Grace Poole's scream (really Bertha's) that follows it somewhat jarring. I agree that it is indeed a *cri de coeur*, but it seems perfectly appropriate to Jane's character and certainly an excellent preface to the cries of the imprisoned mad woman.

[33] The Richardsonian mode is also quite apparent in *Jane Eyre*. Rochester and Jane have a witty duel going between them from their first meeting, but the restoration mode completely takes over during the engagement period when Jane sees her economic dependency upon him as a tremendous threat to her integrity and so she takes to teasing as a defense of her individuality and independence. Which goes to show that even so Byronic a figure as Jane must use the Millamant weapon in the Millamant situation, a situation common to all women.

clear that had the Brontes not been isolated in Yorkshire they would never have been able to write as freely as they did. To have conceived of the sexuality of Jane Eyre is, as Q.D. Leavis has stated,[34] a major imaginative victory in 1848. The Brontes seem to have grown up relatively untouched by the contemporary notions of women's role, although of course their lives were painfully constrained as their brother's never was. But unlike other Victorian women they were aware enough to conceptualize about their constraint. The madness of Bertha and Cathy (at the end of her life) testify to their creators' awareness of what was being choked off, boarded up, violently repressed in their own lives. And it was only their ability to identify with that complete male stereotype, the Bryonic hero, which allowed them to formulate their terrible restlessness into characters who were strong and demanding without being mad.[35] It is not surprising--at least not to me--that the imagination which shaped Jane Eyre boldly proclaiming to Rochester that her passion for him is equal to his for her, should also invent the nightmare image of the hairy, bestial, lurid, screaming, murderous Bertha[36]

---

[34] See her "Preface" to the Penguin edition of Jane Eyre.

[35] See Fanny E. Ratchford, The Brontes' Web of Childhood (New York: Columbia University Press, 1941) for a good account of the way the Brontes' imaginations were fed on their isolation and their reading of Byron's romances and communal Byronic fantasies.

[36] It is worth mentioning that Bertha is not (and indeed

grown crazy after a long course of promiscuity.

The double image of Bertha raging in her locked turret and Clarissa lying drugged and violated are the central alternatives of eroticism presented in English fiction. Clarissa, it will be remembered, scorns wedlock with Lovelace, but she speaks of her death as if it were a wedding and she prepares her coffin as if it were a marriage bed. The alternatives of death-seeking chastity and violent sexuality, of suicide or murder, or adjustment to the prison by regulating your mind and your desires or of smashing against the walls with the strength of your imagination, these are the individual's and particularly the woman's stances imaged in the English novel and in the mythos of middle-class life.

-5-

Meredith works very hard to image another stance. Imagine a "Bertha Harlow," a woman fighting against her own sexuality and against the walls of her prison and you have some idea of the sort of effort Meredith was making. He does not rework the standard formulas--he calls them completely into question, trying to combine elements that the novel had tra-

---

could not be) an English woman. She is even more than French, she is Creole, and presumably part Negro. Rochester's other mistresses are continental European, but for such a woman as this Bronte had to send him to the West Indies.

ditionally separated. More than other novelists, Meredith is fundamentally experimental, shattering the materials he reaches for rather than reshaping them. He does not make his own new blend of the picaresque and the Richardsonian modes; he puts so much pressure on both modes that the whole fabric of fiction-making starts to tear in his hands.

First of all, Meredith does not accept the basic mythic structures of sex and violence which I have outlined above. He takes the victimization out of sexuality, and he also takes the sexuality out of victimization. Such sexuality is repellent to his imagination as well as to his morality. Secondly, his plots are both adventurous and enclosed. The action is generated fairly evenly from within the individual and from the pressures of society. We are accustomed to focusing our attention on one sphere or the other. Either we watch very closely for Clarissa's smallest gesture and most minute movement of the heart, or we take personality for granted and watch to see who is likely to meet Tom Jones at the inn and what they will try to do to him. But the very purposeful randomness of a Meredithian plot calls upon us to watch both fronts at once. We are in suspense lest Richard decide never to return to his wife, and we are in suspense lest he get caught in Mountfalcon's plot. The amount of plain confusion in a Meredith novel, then, is always very high and it takes a great deal of attention to keep the situation of the novel in focus, since it is subject to change from motives of character and from drastic external events.

Finally and most importantly, the ambiguity of moral choices in Meredith marks a wide departure from previous fictional patterns. Pamela and Clarissa have confused motives and are in ambiguous situations. Jane Eyre faces a very difficult choice when she runs away from Thornfield. But in none of these novels do we lose the sense of a definite right and wrong, somewhere beneath the levels of subtle meanings and confusing circumstances. In Meredith's fiction the way out of a difficult situation is always much less clear. He is far more interested in the energy which goes into the choice. In <u>Diana of the Crossways</u>, as we will be seeing, this energy is the primary motive force behind the novel. Meredith in effect moves the discontinuous, chancey world of the picaresque into the inner-centered mode of the Richardsonian novel. He subjects his characters to the kind of scrutiny to which Richardson or Austen subject theirs, but he does so without a firm sense of which way Richard or Clara or Diana should turn at the end of their struggles.

Meredith's stylistic peculiarities are related to this difficult double effort. To put it bluntly, he does not ever know where to put his foot down on solid ground. The archness, pretentiousness, and real affectation which drive many readers away is indeed a function of his refusal to let any attitude go unquestioned. He is never comfortable in one relation to his material. <u>The Egoist</u>, his one attempt at a consistent stance, following the elegant rationale of the "Essay on Comedy," exhausted him.[37] Of course writers of the late nineteenth and early twentieth century were all up against similar uncertainties. But few saw the significance of small social gestures as clearly as Meredith did. He was indeed hypersensitive to the tones of social intercourse. He saw people too minutely to forego the Richardsonian method, and he saw the society too clearly to portray the world as continuous. Hence he is always searching for a comfortable narrative voice and finding one only to break with it and try another. His approach to his creation is tentative in the extreme. And in his suspension he relies especially heavily on literary references as if they were garments to slip on and off, or perhaps more accurately, as if they were all vantage points or lenses for looking at an elusive reality that one can never see completely around. His characteristic style is the mixed metaphor. So "Briareus" and the myth of Diana and the imps of the Comic Spirit, and the "Pilgrim's Scrip" keep obtruding themselves upon his narrative. There is always an ironic distance between him and his creation.[38]

---

[37]See below, Chapter II, p. 85.

[38]Similarly, Meredith's personal life is so shielded

Having acknowledged the many difficulties in reading Meredith, one must add that he is nonetheless bracing. For me, at least, it is always well worth the trouble of tackling the resistence of the surface of Meredith's fiction to come in contact with an imagination so agile, vital, original, and so energetically devoted to the articulation of its own generous vision. I hope that these essays are helpful in increasing the pleasure of the reader in these three extraordinary novels. And for those who can, perhaps in despite of his style, read the novels with pleasure, I would make a plea for the kind of respect that George Meredith deserves, if only for the courage and ingenuity of his failures.

---

from our direct understanding by the personas he adopts in his letters and by the performance quality of his famous witty conversation, that we really cannot tell exactly what is at the bottom of his failure to achieve an even, comfortable tone. None of the biographies of Meredith succeed in communicating a sense of his personality. The living man is incredibly elusive for someone so prolific and in many ways so personal in his public writing. Certainly though Dickens never wrote a novel about his relationship with his wife and his mistress we have a much firmer idea of what he was like as an intimate than we have of the author of <u>The Ordeal of Richard Feverel</u> and "Modern Love."

CHAPTER I

The Ordeal of Richard Feverel: A Novel with a Hero

-1-

> And since the first novel is always apt to be an unguarded one, where the author displays his gifts without knowing how to dispose of them to the best advantage, we may do well to open <u>Richard Feverel</u> first. It needs no great sagacity to see that the writer is a novice at his task. The style is extremely uneven. Now he twists himself into iron knots; now he lies flat as a pancake. He seems to be of two minds as to his intention. Ironic comment alternates with long-winded narrative. He vacillates from one attitude to another. Indeed, the whole fabric seems to rock a little insecurely. The baronet wrapped in a cloak; the county family; the ancestral home; the uncles mouthing epigrams in the diningroom; the great ladies flaunting and swimming; the jolly farmers slapping their thighs; all liberally if spasmodically sprinkled with dried aphorisms from a pepper-pot called the Pilgrim's Scrip--what an odd conglomeration it is! But the oddity is not on the surface; it is not merely that whiskers and bonnets have gone out of fashion; it lies deeper, in Meredith's intention, in what he wishes to bring to pass. He has been, it is plain, at great pains to destroy the conventional form of the novel. He makes no attempt to preserve the sober reality of Trollope and Jane Austen; he has destroyed all the usual staircases by which we have learnt to climb. And what is done so deliberately is done with a purpose. The defiance of the ordinary, these airs and graces, the formality of the dialogue with its Sirs and Madams are all there to create an atmosphere that is unlike that of daily life, to prepare the way for a new and original sense of the human scene.[1]

As an experimental novelist herself, Virginia Woolf is alert to the significance of Meredith's notorious oddities. His

---

[1] "The Novels of George Meredith" in <u>The Second Common Reader</u> (New York: Harvest Books, 1960), p. 206.

style is indeed difficult and idiosyncratic, but his vacillations represent his difficulty in coming into a new relation to his material. He keeps trying on different styles and discarding them midsentence. And the form of his novels and particularly of his first novel is even more puzzling and disorienting than the style. He "has destroyed all the usual staircases by which we have learnt to climb." He is actually out to "destroy the conventional form of the novel." And why? Because he is anxious to "prepare the way for a new and original sense of the human scene." Woolf refers to Meredith's "defiance of the ordinary," but it is really his defiance of the novelistic which she is talking about. He is indeed out to smash the old stairways that lead to the reality of other English novelists, but are ill-suited to convey his own imaginative vision of the world.

The most obvious departure for the first readers of the novel, in 1859, was the seduction of Richard by the courtesan Bella Mount. This attempt at opening up the Victorian novel to Victorian sexuality was met by the banning of the novel from Mudie's Circulating Library, ensuring its commercial failure. The other major innovation--the unexpected tragic ending of what looks like a romance or a comedy until the final chapters--remains puzzling and disturbing.[2] It is hard

---

[2] This is a persistent theme in criticism of the novel, see for example: Joseph Warren Beach, *The Comic Spirit in*

to know how to take it. In Victorian novels we can accept a sentimental catastrophe like the death of little Paul Dombey, or an effective ironic shock like the death of George Osborne; but Lucy's death at the very end of this novel is distressing and shocking in ways not so easily reconciled by any immediately available sense of literary closure. That is, it doesn't look like anything we've seen anywhere else, and even in context it seems unprepared for and gratuitously painful. Meredith seems to be breaking up his own patterns, disorienting the reader even on the very last page where we expect a resolution, not a blow.

Like many novelists, notably Fielding and Austen, who are both invoked in Richard Feverel,[3] Meredith is beginning his career by reacting against other novels. Shamela and Northanger Abbey were parodies which allowed their writers to go forward past the accepted premises of fiction which they

---

George Meredith: An Interpretation (New York: 1911), Chapter III; Walter F. Wright, Art and Substance in George Meredith: A Study in Narrative (Nebraska: 1953), Chapter VIII; and for the most assertive and wrongheaded expression of disappointment see John W. Morris, "Inherent Principles of Order in Richard Feverel," PMLA, 76 (1963), pp. 333-340. The controversy is summarized in I.M. Williams, "The Organic Structure of The Ordeal of Richard Feverel," RES, 18 (1967), pp. 16-29. Williams largely acknowledges the structural integrity of the novel, although he, too, faults Meredith for inconsistencies.

[3]See p. 57 below for Meredith's debt to Fielding. It seems significant to me that Meredith chooses the names "Austin" and "Wentworth" (the name of the captain in Persuasion) for his characters.

were violently rejecting. In <u>Richard Peverel</u> Meredith is making a similar effort. Just as Jane Austen had to exorcise the soppiness of the Gothic heroine and the unreality of the Gothic world in order to clear the way for her own vision, so Meredith had to confront and break apart the accepted courtship patterns of English fiction and the accepted virtues and vices of English heroes and heroines, and most of all the sentimentality of the Victorian novel in order to clear a space for his own reality. In reading Meredith's fiction, then, and especially his first novel, we must be prepared to be jarred, unsettled, disturbed, and puzzled. He has set out to "destroy the conventional form of the novel" becuase he wants to shake his readers out of the comfortable assumptions those forms confirm; he offers instead new patterns, new ways of construing our experience. And we must be willing to feel rather lost in order to make ourselves available for Meredith's "new and original sense of the human scene."

-2-

It is useful to begin a discussion of such a disorienting novel by ordering its complicated action into the three discreet sections which I think are quite obviously the units in which it was conceived.

In 1858 Meredith's wife, Mary Peacock Nicoll Meredith,

deserted him and their five-year-old son, and eloped with her lover to Italy. The following year The Ordeal of Richard Feverel was published. It tells the story of Sir Austin Feverel who is similarly deserted by another Mary and left with an infant son, Richard.[4] When his wife leaves him Sir Austin writes a book of aphorisms, "The Pilgrim's Scrip," on the eternal treachery of Eve, and he formulates a scientific "System" to prepare his son to meet her temptation, which he thinks of as the family Ordeal. The novel describes the failure of Sir Austin's System, beginning with Richard's fourteenth birthday when he gets into his first big scrape and ending approximately on his twenty-first birthday when he is left like his father with an infant son to raise alone.

Richard runs away from his fourteenth birtday celebration rather than strip for a medical examination. He quixotically tramps across the countryside looking for adventure with his new Sancho Panza comrade, Ripton, and runs into Farmer Blaize who whips the boys for poaching. Because the delicately reared Richard cannot bear the indignity of the whip-

---

[4] It is important to note the biographical basis for the novel. It is hard to believe that Meredith is writing from so fresh a wound, especially since Sir Austin is close to being the villain of the piece. Mary and her lover are shadowy pathetic figures. The detachment is hard won and clearly an emotional purgative of some sort for Meredith. Gillian Beer's discussion of the novel in Meredith: A Change of Masks (London: Athlone Press, 1970) centers around Meredith's moral courage in writing it.

ping, he hires Tom Bakewell, a plowboy, to burn the farmer's rick in retaliation. A series of juvenile plots and adult counter-plots eventually lead to Richard's confession and repentance. This first section of the novel is referred to by the narrator as The Bakewell Comedy.

In the second section of the novel the "Son of a System" reaches adolescence, and falls in love with Farmer Blaize's niece Lucy, while Sir Austin is off in London scientifically seeking a mate for the boy. The lovers are discovered and separated, and Richard falls into total apathy. In an effort to restore the boy's spirits the Baronet sends him up to London where he accidentally finds Lucy, and, in a burst of impetuous love and defiance, convinces her to elope. The couple are secretly married and go to the Isle of Wight for their honeymoon.

With the marriage, Richard has crossed his "Rubicon" into adulthood and the rest of the novel is increasingly serious and ominous. Sir Austin is so hurt by his beloved son's disobedience and by the apparent failure of the System that he refuses to be reconciled. But Lucy is informed by Richard's cynical young cousin and tutor Adrian that Sir Austin would probably agree to see Richard alone. In compassion for her husband, Lucy pretends that she is afraid to meet Sir Austin and convinces Richard to go alone to London, where Adrian, under instructions from Sir Austin, takes him into "every sort of company." The Baronet remains sulking on a mountaintop in Wales pretending to have a plan and waiting for time to heal his resentment.

The results are catastrophic. Richard's ignorance of women leaves him an easy prey to Bella Mount who allows him to think he is reforming her. His seduction sends him into such a pit of self-hatred that when Sir Austin does arrive in London finally offering to reunite him with his wife, Richard no longer feels worthy of her. Furthermore, while he is fighting with his love and his shame, Richard is called to the deathbed of his adoring cousin Clare. She leaves a diary detailing her girlish love for him and her agony at his scorn of her loveless arranged marriage. Richard feels responsible for her death and byronically exiles himself from England in self-hatred and shame. Lucy, left alone on the Isle of Wight, has a son unknown to her husband and unrecognized by Sir Austin.

At this point in the action Richard's responsible and selfless cousin Austin Wentworth returns to England after a long absence. He takes Lucy and the child to Sir Austin immediately, knowing that the Baronet will receive them if his pride is spared the pain of inviting them himself. Wentworth then searches out Richard and tells him he is a father. A Rhineland forest storm awakens in Richard a religious awe of his abandoned wife and child and leaves him purified and ready to return to love and duty in England.

All seems well. Richard is returning. Sir Austin and
Lucy await him together at Raynham. Then Richard stops at
his London hotel and finds an old letter from Bella telling
him of a plot against his wife on the part of Bella's old
paramour Lord Mountfalcon. He feels compelled to challenge
the dissolute lord to a duel. The duel is arranged for the
next day. Richard goes home for only an hour, tortured by
the necessity to leave his wife and child again. He leaves
Lucy near distraction with fear, and embarks for France and
the duel.

The last chapter is a letter describing Lucy's death of
brain fever in France. She has broken under the final strain
of being near her wounded husband but forbidden to see or
speak to him for fear of worsening his condition. It drives
her mad and ultimately kills her. Richard recovers from his
wound a completely shattered man without the wife who had
been the real center of his life. The loving Lady Blandish
laments that "he will never be what he promised." The Hope
of Raynham has fallen victim to the Feverel Ordeal.

Richard is one of the first children in fiction to grow
logically before our eyes, filling out a skeletal character
apparent in his boyhood. The quixotic mistakes which are
comic in the boy and endearingly romantic in the adolescent
are disastrously irresponsible in the adult. The pride and
energy which lead him to arson and elopement lead as well to

the three abortive heroic actions of the final section: the attempt to prevent Clare's marriage which ends in her death; the campaign in aid of fallen women which ends in Richard's seduction; and finally the duel to defend his and Lucy's honor which destroys them both. A careful reading of the novel reveals the deliberateness with which the seeds of the disaster are made apparent in the playful antics of the young man.

The first fourteen chapters of the novel quite deliberately I think bring the boy just past his fourteenth birthday. Chapters I-IV introduce us to Sir Austin, his misogyny, and his System, and so serve as a prologue to the novel as a whole and to the Bakewell Comedy section.[5] The present action of the novel begins in Chapter V which is entitled "Showing How the Fates Selected the Fourteenth Birthday to Try the Strength of the System." The test of the System is presented as a comedy of English boyhood and in fact, as we shall see, owes a great deal to Tom Jones.

The second section of fourteen chapters is the part of the novel most vividly and affectionately remembered by many

---

[5] I have chosen to use the original or 1859 version of the novel, as it is reproduced in The Modern Library edition edited by Lionel Stevenson (1950). There is a textual controversy here, since Meredith made cuts in the novel for the 1878 edition. If only for the sake of the plot points eliminated by Meredith's scissor work I think it is important to rely on the original text. All page references will be to the Modern Library edition.

readers for the lyric romanticism with which the courtship
of Richard and Lucy is described. Chapters XV and XVI serve
as prologue to this section, rapidly summarizing four years
of Richard's life, bringing him to adolescence and establishing Sir Austin's responsibility for Richard's romantic fever,
since it is Sir Austin's flirtation with Lady Blandish which
precipitates Richard's romance with Lucy. The second section
of the novel ends with another birthday rebellion, now at age
nineteen. Richard attempts to find Lucy on a stormy night
and succeeds only in making himself ill. His recuperation
furthers the romance of Sir Austin and Lady Blandish, which
provokes at the very center of the novel the key epigram:
"Sentimentalists are they who seek to enjoy Reality without
incurring the Immense Debtorship for a thing done."

Chapter XXIX begins the "New Comedy" as Meredith calls
this part of the action, reflecting the fact that the elopement is successor to the old Bakewell Comedy. The tag also
puns on the Hellenistic "New Comedy" which presented a pair
of young lovers circumventing the opposition of an old father.
Immediately after the marriage comedy, in Chapter XXXV, the
"Creditor" appears in the form of cousin Adrian who will
announce the "thing done" to the world. The rest of the
novel is concerned with the debtorship incurred by the System
and by the marriage. Sir Austin and Richard are both called
to account and must face up to the consequences of their

sentimental actions.

Tragedy becomes a possibility because Richard is no longer a child. He has undertaken an adult's responsibilities by marrying, and he has come upon adult problems which his father is no longer willing to providentially bail him out of. Through Bella and Clare he gains carnal knowledge and the knowledge of death, so that when he is faced with the final ordeal of choice presented by Bella's letter, he is no longer an ignorant child but a morally responsible adult, capable of tragic error with irrevocable consequences.[6] The changes from comedy to romance to tragedy in the separate sections of the novel are not a wavering of artistic intention, then, but a daring attempt to represent the organic progression of Richard's life from childhood through adolescence and into an adulthood for which he is ill-prepared. Meredith is attempting to write comedy and romance with the

---

[6] Meredith underscores Richard's capacity for choice by carefully making the duel an agonizing matter of chance. We are told that "Richard had a momentary idea of not driving to the hotel" where Bella's letter awaits him (562). Further, "If foolish Ripton had not delayed to tell him of his interview with Mountfalcon all might have been well" (383). No fewer than five characters--Ripton, Adrian, Mrs. Doria, and Richard and Mountfalcon themselves--do not want the duel to take place and have the power to prevent it. The duel is arbitrary, in that it need not have happened; it is Richard who wills the catastrophe by seeking this melodramatic release for his humiliation. Like his meeting with Bella Mount the duel is set in October recalling the recurrent birthday rebellions. At fourteen he fled to avoid undressing; at twenty-nine he flees Raynham again to avoid facing the physical sense of self-loathing and degradation which Bella's letter reawakens in him.

moral force of tragedy, and though that force may not be immediately apparent to his readers he is certainly hoping to move us to a recognition of the seriousness of gestures we view sentimentally as merely funny or romantic. The novel is designed, then, to jar us by the fruits of Richard's boyhood and adolescence and so make us reexamine our original conventional reactions.

-3-

About half way through the novel Meredith pulls himself up short in the midst of describing the hero's departure from his cloistered estate and confronts himself with the fact that he probably has no audience for what he is trying to say. The passage clearly comes out of the self-consciousness which Virginia Woolf shrewdly associates with the beginning novelist, although it speaks to all of Meredith's fiction. Characteristically enough, the tone changes from simple irony directed as Sir Austin watching Richard board the train for London to a genuine plea for a new audience for a new sort of fiction.

> Now surely there will come an Age when the presentation of Science at war with Fortune and the Fates will be deemed the true Epic of modern life; and the aspect of a Scientific Humanist who, by dint of incessant watchfulness, has maintained a System against those active forces, cannot be reckoned less than sublime, even though at the moment he but sit upon his horse, on a fine March morning such as this and smile wistfully to behold the son of his heart, his System incarnate, wave a serene adieu to tutelage,

> neither too eager nor morbidly unwilling to try his
> luck alone for a term of two weeks. At present, I
> am aware, an audience impatient for Blood and Glory
> scorns the stress I am putting on incidents so minute,
> a picture so little imposing. One will come to whom
> it will be given to see the elementary machinery at
> work: who, as it were, from some slight hint of the
> straws, will feel the winds of March when they do
> not blow. To them will nothing be trivial, seeing
> that they will have in their eyes the invisible con-
> flict going on around us, whose features a nod, a
> smile, a laugh of ours perpetually changes. And they
> will perceive, moreover, that in real life all hangs
> together: the train is laid in the lifting of an
> eyebrow, that burst upon the field of thousands.
> They will see the links of things as they pass, and
> wonder not, as foolish people now do, that this
> great matter came out of that small one. (280)

The point at which the paragraph changes tone and subject (but not rhetorical figure) is the description of Richard "neither too eager nor morbidly unwilling to try his luck alone for a term of two weeks." Meredith is here describing the important point of this section of the narrative for he is about to make the temperate Richard laugh uproariously as the train pulls out, planting a seed of distrust in his father's mind which will mature when the trip ends in his elopement. So it is very important to Meredith that we pay attention here to Sir Austin watching Richard get on the train. It is an important link in a novel which above all asks us to make the effort to watch the links as they pass turning innocent pranks into dangerous risks.

But Meredith clearly has a moment of fear here that his readers won't care about Richard's laugh or his father's surprise. It is too small an incident for the lovers of popular

romance whom he immediately invokes. And he is perfectly
right in seeing his effort as ahead of its time. Since Sigmund Freud we are prepared to see "a nod, a smile, a laugh"
as more than a superficial token of social intercourse. Meredith is without Freud, but asking for a similar intensity of
attention to the seemingly trivial details of daily life.
He is looking for clues, really, or for a new sign language
to make concrete the "invisible conflict" that makes up our
social intercourse--invisible because it is private, internal,
and because we lack the language to catch it as it passes.
He is especially astute at recording the ways in which people
change toward one another, something which D.H. Lawrence similarly struggled to articulate half a century later. The invisible conflict, then, is first of all the complexity of
feeling between intimates. Secondly it is a moral conflict--
not the simplistic Manichaean contest the sentimental Sir
Austin imagines--but the subtle, even involuted conflict which
Henry James was later to portray, in which every minute incident of life moves us in many ways as we constantly define
and redefine our responsibilities toward one another. Meredith is right in pulling himself up short as he does here with
the recognition that the effort he is making and more importantly, the effort he is asking of his readers, is extraordinary for the year 1859, and does indeed amount to an effort
to see the invisible. He was right to trust, however, that

what is invisible to one generation can be apparent to the next. Because of his struggle to realize the invisible, subtle flux of the emotional and moral life Meredith had a special hatred for sentimentality and for its mirror image, cynicism. Sir Austin and Adrian represent these false values and their simplistic view of good and evil is an important destructive force in the novel. In Richard, sentimentality takes the form of heroism.

When Meredith uses "heroism" as a pejorative term (which is the only way he does use it) he is thinking first of all of the exaggerated behavior of the heroes of those novels which satisfy the taste for "Blood and Glory" rather than presenting the minute incidents of "real life." Richard parodies such a hero, and like Don Quixote or Catherine Morland (the heroine of <u>Northanger Abbey</u>), he stands as an exemplum of the dangers of imitating romance in reality. Aside from the literary context, Meredith's notion of "Heroism" also entails something for which Meredith had no terms, but which we would now call sex role typing. Of course, fictional heroes and heroines embody cultural ideals of masculine and feminine behavior. Meredith is parodying and exposing both the fictional type and the cultural stereotype. For example, dueling is a particular bête noir of Meredith's which plays a key role in this novel and is undercut both as a staple of fictional heroes (an unrealistic and sentimental approach to complex moral choices) and also as a symbol of what is wrong with cultural expectations of masculinity (false courage based upon overblown notions of pride and possession).

Richard's heroism is the result of the System, which is in turn born of Sir Austin's misogyny. The misogyny, as Meredith shrewdly perceives it, is the result of Sir Austin's inability to deal with what he considers "womanish" in himself--his own vulnerability to emotion:

> "To withstand them [women] must we first annihilate our mothers within us: die half!" [Sir Austin writes in the Pilgrim's Scrip.]
> The poor gentleman seriously believing Woman to be a Mistake, had long been trying to do so. Had he succeeded, he would have died his best half, for his mother was strong in him. The very acridity of the Aphorisms, the GREAT SHADDOCK DOGMA [i.e. Eve's apple] itself, spring from Wounded softness, not from hardness. (10)

The System is itself a giant parody of male sex role typing. Sir Austin attempts to heal his wound by denying its existence. He feigns a manly, philosophic detachment, thinking that manliness and philosophy mean an invulnerability to emotion. He takes refuge behind an exaggerated mask of rationality, which parodies scientific detachment. Further, he projects his emotional nature onto his wife and then onto women in general.[7]

---

[7] It is important to note here that Meredith's response was very different. He wrote not a Pilgrim's Scrip, but this novel, and more importantly, Modern Love (1862), a sequence of poems which describes the breakdown of a marriage, ascrib-

Meredith demonstrates the absurdity of Sir Austin's solution by emphasizing his condemnation of <u>all</u> women and of sexuality itself. But it is quite clear to Meredith that Sir Austin is merely making an apple into a grapefruit (that is, a shaddock), so to speak: merely taking the Eden myth a little more seriously than we are accustomed to take it. But the myth itself, as Meredith sees quite well, is a fundamental expression of the pervasive Western distrust of the female, and Sir Austin's System is but a logical exaggeration of our cultural expectations of male and female behavior.

The workings of heroism and pride in men is the larger moral focus of the novel. It is revealed in gestures, in minute incidents like Sir Austin's dismissal of the nurse who sees him crying over his son's bed; like Richard's refusal to undress for a doctor--the first sign of the morbid pride fostered by his secluded upbringing; like Richard's burning of Farmer Blaize's rick in the violence of his response to a whipping. Meredith informs each of these gestures with the weight of moral choice.

Richard's apology to Farmer Blaize is a good example of Meredith's meticulous weighting of details and his distrust of the conventionally heroic. Richard has promised his good cousin Austin Wentworth that he will stop trying to get Tom

---

ing the blame quite clearly to the husband as well as to the adulterous wife.

Bakewell out of jail with a rope and a file, and go and ask
Farmer Blaize to please not prosecute. Richard manages to
get through a simple apology to the hated farmer, but he
cannot bring himself to ask an enemy for a favor. His words
are like a bitter drink he cannot swallow:

> The draught grew more and more abhorrent. To proclaim one's iniquity; to apologize for one's wrongdoing: Thus much could be done: but to beg a favour of the offended party--that was beyond the self-abasement any Feverel could consent to. Pride, however, whose inevitable battle is against itself, drew aside the curtains of poor Tom's prison, crying a second time, "Behold your benefactor!" and with the words burning in his ears Richard swallowed the dose:
> "Well, then! I want you, Mr. Blaize,--if you don't mind--will you help me to get this man Bakewell off his punishment." (96)

In the fun of Richard's elaborate attempts to phrase
the request to the confused farmer it is easy to overlook
the subtle moral test Meredith has constructed for the boy.
He has made the assumption that there is no great virtue in
Richard's refusal to let Tom suffer for his offense. The boy's
pride would not allow him to accept such a favor from a mere
ploughman; it would be too humiliating. Furthermore, Meredith makes light of the apology to Farmer Blaize, since to
apologize for an acknowledged wrong is not an undignified act,
especially since Richard is ready to pay the farmer off,
making the apology at least partially a gesture of patrician
magnanimity. Richard's real test--the minute gesture worth
watching for--is the necessity to do something truly painful

and humiliating in order to fulfill his responsibility to
Tom. And here his pride and his sense of being a Feverel
(always a pejorative term in the novel) intervene between
him and the truly honorable act. He winds up able to make
the gesture only because it would be more humiliating not to
make it. Richard saves Tom Bakewell from transportation because he is too proud to remain in Tom's debt. It is his
pride not his moral sense at all which leads him to do the
right thing.

The poaching/whipping incident is adapted from Tom
Jones' boyhood scrape with Black George.[8] In Fielding's
novel Tom's "natural goodness of heart" is demonstrated by
his willingness to submit to a whipping rather than peach
on a friend (a gesture much like Tom Bakewell's toward
Richard). Meredith takes such boyish loyalty almost for
granted, and values instead the good action which is not so
dramtically valid to the imagination of a boy.

Richard is a very engaging boy--as engaging as Tom
Jones and in many of the same ways. But Meredith expects a
much more complex reaction from his reader than Fielding did.
Meredith expects us to be aware that Richard's willingness
to rescue Tom with a rope and pulley from the jail, charming

---

[8] Book III, Chapters 2-4. Tom takes a brutal whipping rather than involve the gamekeeper Black George in his offense. Tom's English pluck and energy and Fielding's affectionate enjoyment of his "hero's" boyish quixotry are clearly behind Meredith's depiction of Richard's boyhood.

gallantry that it is, is an ominous sign that he is too
proud, too heroic, too much a Feverel, to accept human solu-
tions to his problems. This is the very character trait
which leads him to the final disastrous duel, and so the apology to Farmer Blaize is one of the minute "invisible links"
that will lead to the "great thing" of Richard's Ordeal.
We are to see the young Richard as a "barbarian as to right
and wrong" while Fielding wants us to see Tom's "natural
goodness of heart"--as if the moral life were not composed
of many subtle invisible links, but were all of one piece
from birth. Meredith wants us to differentiate between the
boyish virtues (which become the barbaric or heroic virtues
of manhood) such as not peaching on a friend, and the true
adult virtues such as the ability to accept humiliation.
The first is the acceptable province of the hero; the second
is a great deal harder to deal with in novels and in life.

It should be clear, then, that Meredith is making his
light comedy of boyhood scrapes carry a great deal of moral
freight, and demanding that his readers see the subtle moral
choices involved in the slapstick and mock-heroism of the
narrative. The romantic section of the novel is equally demanding, although in a different way. In the second fourteen
chapters of the novel Meredith juxtaposes Sir Austin's foolish scientific search for a mate with the work of the "in-
stincts" in bringing Lucy and Richard together. The courtship

is described in lyric passages which call on resonances of Wordsworth, Shakespeare (particularly *The Tempest*), classical pastorals, Arthurian romance, and fairy tale. The tone is so distinctive and the resonances are so dense because Meredith is trying to capture a very special sense of the moral and emotional state of these "instinctual" adolescents--a state which is emblematic to him of much more than the simple young love he keeps telling us he is describing in such stylized language.

In the romance section of the novel[9] Meredith has developed a precise idiom for conveying the beauty and the extreme fragility of Richard's and Lucy's love. He calls upon many literary associations because he wants us to feel the essential artificiality and ephemerality of their innocent passion. He sees this stage of their lives as a real Eden. Their innocence is genuine although it is an artificial situation. Their moment of innocence is founded upon

---

[9]Chapters XV-XXVIII, which take Richard from early adolescence through his courtship with Lucy, form a narrative block, like the Bakewell Comedy sequence (Chapters IV-XIV). Within this "romance section" as I am calling it, are all the country love scenes, the contrasting scenes of Sir Austin combing London for a mate for Richard, and Sir Austin's success in separating the lovers. The section begins and ends with the flirtation between Lady Blandish and Sir Austin, which precipitates Richard's infatuation with Lucy. Chapter XXIX begins the "New Comedy" section which depicts Richard's elopement, ending with the marriage ceremony which takes place in Chapter XXXIII, entitled "In Which the Last Act of a Comedy Takes the Place of the First." Chapter XXXIV appropriately opens with Lucy weeping.

ignorance sustainable only by isolation from the rest of the world such as they experience at Raynham, and within the equally short boundaries of their early youth. Their love is associated with the dawn and the sunset; moments of intense but fleeting beauty.

Sir Austin and Lady Blandish also talk of Camelot in a sunset scene, but for them chivalric rhetoric marks the sentimentality of their attachment. For Richard and Lucy it is appropriate because, brought up in seclusion, he at Raynham, she in a convent, they have no sordid associations with sexuality (such as the quite average lad Ripton parades for us in this section); in fact they have been taught to spiritualize all their emotions. We are meant to admire Ferdinand and Miranda as much as they admire each other; like Lady Blandish we are to be half in love with them ourselves. But we are also supposed to perceive the transitory nature of the Camelot they are living in:

> The shadow of the Cypress was lessening on the lake. The moon was climbing high. As Richard rowed the boat, Lucy sung to him softly. She sang first a fresh little French song; reminding him of a day when she had been asked to sing to him before, and he did not care to hear. "Did I live?" he thinks. Then she sang to him a bit of one of those majestic old Gregorian chants, that whenever you may hear them, seem to build up cathedral walls around you. The young man dropped the sculls. The strange solemn notes gave a religious tone to his love, wafted him into the Knightly Ages and the reverential Heart of Chivalry.
> Hanging between two Heavens on the lake: floating to her voice: the moon stepping over and through white shoals of soft high clouds above, and below:

>   floating to her voice--no other breath abroad!
>   His soul went out of his body as he listened.
>   They must part. He rows her gently shore-
>   ward.   (211-212)

The very fragility of the scene is moving. The reader is drawn into Richard's ecstacy on the lake and feels with him the cathedral walls building around him. But while we experience this Wordsworthian spot of time in the middle of the lake we are also seeing forward with the shadow of the Cypress (a symbol of the Feverel curse throughout the novel, and one which is picked up in the conversation which follows this passage) and backwards to the Bakewell Comedy with Richard's dim memory of the night of the bitter draught when he declined to hear Lucy sing. The intense delicacy of this Camelot is further disrupted by Richard's leaving this double heaven to mercilessly beat Benson the butler who has been spying upon the lovers. Richard's chivalry as a lover is as naive and potentially destructive as the gallantry of the comic section.

The winds of march have been blowing through the first two sections of the novel, although they blow in vain for a great many readers. But the readers Meredith hoped for will have seen throughout Richard's simple, scampish boyhood and throughout his instinctual, innocent courtship an invisible conflict going on and will not wonder when the novel turns darker that this great matter should have come of these small ones.

-4-

The romance section of the novel begins and ends with Sir Austin kissing Lady Blandish's hand, perhaps to emphasize the father's role in forming the romantic life of the son. The second kiss provokes the central epigram of the novel, ironically put into the mouth of Sir Austin himself:

> "Sentimentalists,' says THE PILGRIM's SCRIP, are they who seek to enjoy Reality without incurring the Immense Debtorship for a thing done."
> "It is," the writer says of Sentimentalism elsewhere, "a happy pastime and an important science to the timid, the idle, and the heartless: but a damning one to them who have anything to forfeit."   (266-7

Clearly the rest of the novel--the final twenty-one chapters beginning with the New Comedy of the elopement--is about the paying off of the debts incurred by Sir Austin and his son. The mock-heroic comedy of Richard's boyhood and the chivalric fantasy of his early youth are played over again in the elopement sequence, gradually modulating into a more and more ominous mode. For instance, here are the marriage vows of the young lovers:

> Firmly the bridegroom tells forth his words. This hour of the complacent Giant [i.e. "Hebrew Time"] at least is his, and that he means to hold him bound through the Eternities, men may hear. Clearly, and with brave modesty, speaks she: no less firmly, though her body trembles: her voice just vibrating while the tone travels, like a smitten vase.
> Time hears the sentence pronounced on him: the frail hands bind his huge limbs and lock the chains. He is used to it: he lets them do as they will.

Richard plotting the elopement may display "princely superiority to truth and heroic promise of overriding all our laws" (297) but Richard taking the irrevocable step, "crossing the River of his Ordeal" (331) without knowing it, is a pathetic innocent in the grip of an implacable, usurious Giant.

It is not accidental that Meredith makes the marriage this important Rubicon, and sets it in the center of the novel rather than in its traditional place at the end. Like Thackeray in *Vanity Fair* Meredith is explicitly playing off our expectations of a marriage as the unquestioned resolution of a narrative and, by implication, of life's adventures.[10] The title of the marriage chapter, "In Which the Last Act of a Comedy Takes the Place of the First," makes the point for us that the New Comedy is over and with it the comedy of Richard's life. Although Richard is as comically and romantically heroic as he was before, the reader is expected to become more and more distressed by the behavior, as it becomes increasingly apparent that the marriage is the beginning of Richard's true Ordeal.

It is in the elopement section that Richard becomes strongly identified as "The Hero." It is an affectionate but still a pejorative term meant to indicate the fellow likely to "override all our laws" in his egoistic and ruthless pursuit of his own aims. We are asked to note his

---

[10] It is not irrelevant to note that both men had particularly bitter personal reasons to know better.

disregard for the "quiet wretches dragged along with him at his chariot wheels" (268). Richard is certainly not the first such parody Hero: Lord Byron himself created Don Juan after too heavy a dose of corsairs and giaours had stirred his sense of humor about himself. In the Victorian novel itself, Steerforth (in _David Copperfield_) and George Osborne (in _Vanity Fair,_ subtitled "A Novel Without a Hero") personify the anti-social impulses and the ugly selfishness which the English typically perceive and distrust in heroism. But Richard, although he is meant to parody the romance hero, is unique in the special associations of his heroism. Unlike Thackeray and Dickens, Meredith does not focus on the sexual vanity of the heroic figure. Unlike all the other Heroes, real and parodic, Richard is not a seducer. He has no aggressive sexual energy, and so he is completely incapable of abusing Little Em'ly or abandoning Amelia Sedley. In this novel, unlike any other that I know of, heroism takes the place of aggressive sexuality as the characteristic masculine vice.

To understand this transformation and the importance of Meredith's vision in its own time it is useful to take a short look at Thackeray's _Pendennis_ (1848-50) which seems to have suggested much of the original framework of the novel. _Pendennis_ is also a "novel without a hero" in that it sets out to tell the story of an Everyman, "with faults and shortcomings, who does not claim to be a hero but only a man and a brother."[11] Like Richard, Arthur Pendennis is raised in seclusion to avoid the corruption of the schools. He is "Prince of Fairoaks" as Richard is "Prince of Raynham" although the sentimentality and adulation of Pen's domain comes from a household entirely female, just as Richard's is purposely almost wholly male. Pen goes to London, makes a friend named Warburton[12] and through his influence and that of Pen's doting mother Helen and his mother's ward Laura, Pen weathers the temptations of the city and discovers his true happiness in seclusion back on his family estate marrried to Laura. Thackeray, like Meredith, was looking back to *Tom Jones* in trying to write his story of an average young man, and as a Victorian he chafed at the loss of freedom the novelist had suffered over the course of a century:

> Even the gentlemen of our age--this is an attempt to describe one of them, no better nor worse than most educated men--even these we cannot show as they are, with the notorious foibles and selfishness of their lives and their education. Since the author of Tom Jones was buried, no writer of fiction among us has been permitted to depict to his utmost power a MAN. We must drape him and give him a certain conventional

---

[11] *Pendennis* (London: Smith, Elder, 1883).

[12] Warburton seems to be the original of Austin Wentworth. Both represent young father figures; their ascetism and rationality is very similar; and they have the same marital history which blights their lives by allying them to lower class uneducated women whom they cannot live with but are too honorable to have deserted.

simper.[13]

Thackeray wrote this in the Preface to the first bound edition of <u>Pendennis</u> (1850) published after the serialized version had provoked cries of indecency over the Fanny Bolton incident. This notorious section contains not so much as a stolen kiss, but merely a plausible opportunity for Pen to seduce a lower-class innocent girl. The situation is hardly shocking today, but ironically enough it is rather shocking to watch the conventional simper with which Pen fights off temptation. Here is Richard Feverel's prototype responding to an accusation that he has improper designs upon young Fanny:

> ". . . I did not imagine that I had made an impression on poor Fanny until--until tonight. And then, sir, as you came upon me. And," he added with a glow upon his cheek, which in the gathering darkness his companion could not see, and with an audible tremor in his voice, "I do not mind telling you, sir, that on this sabbath evening, as the church bells were ringing, I thought of my own home, and of women angelically pure and good, who dwell there; and I was running hither, as I met you, that I might avoid the danger which be- [14] sets me, and ask strength of God Almighty to do my duty.

Pen does not so much rise above temptation as fall below it. Because of passages like this one, we never truly believe that Pen is a "MAN"--or even an ordinary "man." It is significant that Richard Feverel is never expected to guard his chastity with a conventional simper, nor to curb his sexual energy

---

[13] Vol. I, iv.

[14] Vol. II, 246-7.

by running away from temptation. Meredith assumes that seducing Fanny Bolton (like peaching on a friend) is an act which mere pride rather than virtue would prevent.

Richard is also very believably a MAN. He has an authentic sexuality which is very rare in the Victorian novel. Mrs. Berry points out that he is seduced by Bella Mount partly because he is "warm from a young marriage" (527); and despite the angelic epithets lavished upon Lucy, the marriage is indeed explicitly sexual. Here is our first view of the couple after their elopement:

> By an open window that looked on the brine through nodding roses, our young bridal pair were at breakfast, regaling worthily both of them. Had the Scientific Humanist observed them, he could not have contested the fact that as a couple who had set up to be father and mother of Britons, they were doing their duty. Piles of egg-cups with disintegrated shells bore witness to it, and they were still at work, hardly talking from rapidity of exercise. . . . At times a chance word might spring a laugh, but eating was the business of the hour, as I would have you to know it always will be where Cupid is in earnest. Neglected lies Love's penny-whistle the pastoral flute invoked in the romance chapters on which they played so prettily, and charmed the spheres to hear them. What do they care for the spheres who have one another? Come eggs! come bread and butter! come tea with sugar in it and milk! and welcome the jolly hours. That is a fair interpretation of the music in them just now. Yonder instrument was good only for the Overture. (399)[15]

Richard's and Lucy's sexuality is celebrated as part of their blooming health and beauty. In this delightfully witty and

---

[15]This is a tricky passage, full of the stylistic extravagance that often irritates readers of Meredith. But it is a

proper passage of peculiarly English earthiness, sexuality becomes the duty of married Britons. Passion becomes as wholesome and domestic as a tray of eggs. Of course the broken eggs carry their own association, but the scene itself, like Mrs. Berry's repeated references to the pleasures of the marriage bed, is absolutely chaste. Consummation is celebrated as robust, rendering infatuation effete, and releasing a stronger passion. Similarly, Meredith makes explicit Richard's sexual desires for Lucy during their separation, desires which keep pulling him <u>away</u> from Bella and back to the Isle of Wight. Here he is conjuring up his wife's image as she looks in lovemaking:

> "Talk on, dear old Rip! She's my darling love, whatever she is! And she is gloriously lovely. No eyes like hers. And when I make them bashful-- by Heaven! I'll go down tomorrow the first thing.(461)

Compare this to Pendennis' experience of Laura's first embrace as "arms as tender as Helen's his dead mother! once more enfold him."[16] In an age in which the Oedipal urge is

---

good example of the frequent root of that extravagance in the struggle to express a novel or idiosyncratic vision of experience. Here Meredith is trying to establish their sexuality, something his audience is not really ready to hear, and so he is uneasy and goes about it from many directions at once trying to distance himself from them while still enjoying their vitality.

[16]Vol II, 460. In Thackeray the Oedipal pattern is particularly overt, most astoundingly so in <u>Henry Esmond</u> where the hero does indeed marry his step-mother.

that close to the surface turning marriage into a retreat to womb, Meredith is making an enormous leap in presenting marriage as a healthy sexual experience. Richard's sexuality, like his sense of humor, is always on the side of common sense and wholesomeness.

It is his heroism which is the unwholesome influence in Richard's life and results in the catastrophic estrangement of bridegroom and bride. It is indeed his seduction by Bella[17] which takes him from Lucy and provokes the fatal duel, but Meredith is careful to make the seduction the result of heroic pride rather than of concupiscence. For when the penny-whistle romance goes out of Richard's romance with Lucy in favor of bread and butter consummation he becomes anxious not for another woman, but for another field for his heroic fantasies. The seduction is preceded by a restlessness which is not at all erotic.

In a sunset scene on the Isle of Wight Richard is first drawn into an imaginary "little knight-errant infidelity" by Lady Judith Felle's encouragement of him to become "the rescuer and succourer of distressed dames and damsels"—that is, of fallen women.[18] In London, Richard walks the streets with-

---

[17] The role reversal between Richard and Bella is interesting. She dresses like a man, tricks him like a regular Lovelace, and is even compared to Richard III wooing Ann by Meredith's use of the refrain, "Was ever hero in this manner wooed? Was ever hero in this manner won?"

[18] pp. 414-415. Adrian considers Lady Judith "a second

out a purpose and dreams of rehabilitating street-walkers. His lack of familiarity with women makes him morbidly sensitive to the repeated discovery that (in Adrian's cynical words) a passerby "is not the Saint he deems it is the portion of every creature wearing petticoats to be" (443). He wants to open a house for the regeneration of the "divine beings" who have been "betrayed by Love" (456).[19] Like Sir Austin he feels that he has come upon "the root of all evil in the world," only Richard takes it to be not women's inherent evilness, but man's inherent brutality toward women. He develops an equally unnatural System.

> The Lady of the day [Bella] had not been thrown into the Hero's path without an object, he said; and he was sadly right there. He did not express the thing clearly; nevertheless Ripton understood

---

edition of the Blandish" (413) and Richard's twilight conversations with her here and in the Rhineland later are meant to remind us of the sentimental dialogues in which Lady Blandish flirts with Sir Austin with similarly vague flattering speeches.

[19] Richard's sentimental rhetoric is barely more absurd than Charles Dickens' on the same very Victorian theme. In a correspondence with the Baroness Burdett-Coutts on her plans for the establishment of such an institution as Richard plans, Dickens readily speculates on the best ways to induce "the most rigid order, punctuality, and neatness" while simulating the atmosphere of an "innocently cheerful Family" so that a "penitent creature" could achieve a "Return to Happiness" and then be transported to serve as a colonial wife. Meredith is choosing a very vulnerable area of Victorian sentimentalism. (See Dickens' pamphlet and letters on this subject in <u>Letters of Charles Dickens to the Baroness Burdett-Coutts</u>, ed. Charles C. Osborne (London: John Murray, 1931).

> him to mean that he intended to rescue that lady,
> and then other ladies unknown were to be rescued.
> Ripton was to help. He and Ripton were to be the
> knights of this enterprise.   (457)

The tone of the passage and the presence of the shivering Ripton recall the Bakewell Comedy. The scheme, as heroically senseless as the arson and as dangerous, is the offspring of his father's equally presumptuous, nonsensical, and sanctimonious scheme with Richard.

Richard is lured from Lucy, then, not through simple sexual desire, but through the vanity of his heroic egoism. With the infatuation at an end, he looks for a new scenario for knighthood and falls right into Bella's trap. The simple healthy robust pleasures of marriage do not hold his imagination, they do not suit his Feverel pride. The disillusionment of Lucy's pretended cowardice, and worse, the frustration and humiliation of his father's rejection are blows to his self-esteem and to his fantasy life which Richard cannot tolerate. He was extricated from the arson by his father's intervention; he expects the marriage comedy to end the same way. And most of all he expects always to be the lucky, esteemed hero of his own life. He has no experience of any other role.

The awkwardness of a runaway match injures his pride, and, like his father, when his pride is injured, Richard makes up elaborate schemes of power and control to soothe himself. But his imagined heroism only makes his more complex reality all the harder to bear:

> He began to think that the life lying behind him was the life of a fool. What had he done in it? He had burnt a rick and got married! He associated the two facts of his existence. Where was the hero he was to have carved out of Tom Bakewell?-- a wretch he had taught to lie and chicane: and for what? Great Heavens! how ignoble a flash from the light of his aspirations made his marriage appear! (474)

Meredith makes clear that it is Richard's inability to resolve the situation with his father which makes him restlessly turn to the schemes of saving Bella. His inability to find the proper dragon to slay to release her teaches him his "impotence" and demoralizes him further (485). He resigns himself to returning to his wife in these terms:

> "There's nothing better for me!" the Hero groaned. His great ambition must be covered by a house-top: he and the cat must warm themselves on the domestic hearth! The Hero was not aware that his heart moved him to this. His heart was not now in open communion with his mind. (486)

It is on the eve of this defeated return that Richard is seduced by the serpentine Bella and so self-banished from his eden; the innocence and the heroism his father has so carefully nurtured cause him to fall.[20]

---

[20] The seduction is the Fall in the self-conscious Eden references of the novel. Richard is brought up to be a "Tree of Eden" innocent of moral knowledge, with Sir Austin playing the role of "Providence" to his son. After Richard leaves Raynham he falls into the clutches of "Hebrew Time" who officiates at the wedding, marking his departure from the changeless world into the world of consequences. The Golden Bride ballad introduced in Chapter XXVIII associates

Just as important, the same heroism causes what is perhaps his real sin--the morbid overreaction which keeps him from his wife, barred by his own fiery angel from returning to his real happiness. Because Meredith scorns the easy Victorian equation of sin with sexuality he sees through to Richard's more complex problem: he "is one whose body had been made a temple to him and it is desecrated." This reaction has been prepared for by his childhood priggishness, but it takes Meredith's sharp eye to make the further link between that priggishness and byronic satanism. For the same feeling of desecration which drove him from the medical examination at fourteen drives him to his despairing, self-indulgent byronic exile.[21] Richard sins more in his heroic reaction to the seduction than in the seduction itself.

Richard's final reaction to the seduction is the duel with Mountfalcon, which is really the last in a series of

---

Lucy with Eden. Bella is identified with the serpent. Notice that Clare's death is almost concurrent with the seduction. Richard learns about sin and death and then exiles himself, specifically eastward and only returns after his baptism in the Rhine forest. After the fall and the baptism Richard has the ability to choose between good and evil consciously and when he is faced with the choice of reentering Raynham and reclaiming his Golden Bride or fighting the duel, he consciously "summons the powers of Hell" in order to be able to leave.

[21] The title of Chapter XLVIII, "Again the Magian Conflict" refers to Chapter VI "The Magian Conflict," and "The Last Scene" parallels Chapter XIV and Chapter XXIII which close the two comedies.

duels. For Richard, as questing knight has been dueling all
his life. His first impulse when he is whipped by Farmer
Blaize is to challenge him to a duel. The Mounfalcon duel
is parallel to the Bakewell Comedy in many ways, most significantly in the central emotional situation. "The horrible
sense of shame, self-loathing, universal hatred, impotent
vengeance, as if the spirit were steeped in abysmal blackness"
leads him to yearn for a "sweeping and consummate vengeance"
on Farmer Blaize (51). Similarly the revelation of Bella's
letter "scarce left him the feelings of a man when he thought
of it" provoking a "mad pleasure in the prospect of wreaking
[sic] vengeance upon the villain" which "blackened his
brain" (580, 585). The Bakewell Comedy sets up the scenario
for Richard's life. He is led into his marriage, seduction,
and the duel in parallel incidents of impulsive action arising
from feelings of impotence. The whipping, his suspicions
of his father's plot to marry Lucy to Blaize's nephew, the
futility of a life of only rick-burning and marriage, the
degredation of his seduction, each in turn threaten his view
of himself as a hero and so provoke him to increasingly
dangerous futile heroics. Bred to think of himself as pure
and omnipotent, without any occasion for finding out "what
he was made of," Richard falls apart in the larger world of
experience from his inability to come to terms with his own
corruption and impotence.

It is significant that Meredith changed Pendennis' female retinue to a misogynist male household. For he clearly saw a certain kind of heroism as the result not of maternal coddling but of male narcissism. Richard is initiated by his father into an exaggerated male value system which makes him incapable of dealing with his own emotions by raising an image of himself which he can never live up to. Richard's attempts to be the Prince of Raynham turn him into a self-absorbed egoist. His sexuality on the other hand, which is traditionally associated with male aggression, always turns him toward healthy and responsible behavior. The terrible painful bedroom scene before the duel makes this pressingly real. Richard's desire to sleep with his beautiful wife is opposed to his commitment to the duel. The opposition marks Meredith's surprising advance over the standard myths of English fiction, and especially of the Victorian novel. Almost alone of the English novelists, Meredith is capable of perceiving a sexuality divorced from power.

-5-

Meredith's innovative sense of male heroism is matched by his reworking of the Victorian heroine. The transformation of Helen Pendennis and Laura Bell into Mrs. Doria and Clare is a stunning example. Laura Bell is a common type

type of fictional heroine: the pure, domestic, secretly devoted girl who awaits the return of the errant hero and is finally rewarded for her willingness to remain his sexless spinster servant by becoming his wife. Fanny Price in <u>Mansfield Park</u> and Agnes in <u>David Copperfield</u> are good examples of the type. Laura is so maternal a character that as we have seen she is practically identified with Pen's mother, and is certainly identified over and over again as an angel. Laura does see Pen's faults, as his angelic mother cannot, but she manages to worship him anyway. Like Agnes she sees the hero through other false attractions until he finally arrives at the moral stature necessary for him to value her. Fanny, Agnes, Laura, and Clare Doria all love the hero from childhood on, and remain true to their idolatry even when he rejects them in favor of more sexually attractive women.

Clare's unwholesome disposition is a comment upon the realism of such a one-sided courtship. Unrequited love cherished by a girl in restricted circumstances (none of these young women has a full set of parents or financial security) does not make for a healthy personality. Clare's vulnerability and her girlish attachment to Richard is pathetic and moving, but Meredith lays bare the underlying masochism and lack of imagination that would have to be part of such self-denying heroism. Clare's emotional infantilism

and her dutiful will-lessness are parodies of conventional
female virtues. Richard is revolted by her. As a boy he
takes her love for legitimate "tribute" (135), and as a man
he thinks of her as "that wretched slave" (433). Of course
Richard's brutality to Clare exposes his heroic blindness,
and Mrs. Doria's enslavement of her daughter is a damning
parallel to Sir Austin's System. But Clare's victimization
does not win our respect for her, primarily because she has
so little respect for herself. Thackeray saw the unattractiveness of martydom in his portrait of the tedious Amelia
Sedley, but he still warmed to her each time he saw her
extreme helplessness. Meredith is much more distant from
Clare. Her dependency is described almost as a psychosis.
Unlike her angelic prototypes, Clare does not have God on her
side in her passive suffering; Meredith has her write in her
diary that "God never looks on me," because he sees her
idolatrous personality as deeply self-estranged, self-hating
(534).

Furthermore, Clare is not denied sexuality as Laura
Bell is. It is only after her death that Richard is allowed
to see her as a heavenly judge of his behavior, a Victorian
angel. Richard awakens Clare to her own strong sexuality by
kissing her on the mouth at their final interview before her
marriage. It is this kiss and the knowledge of Richard's
revulsion at what he sees as her prostitution of herself to

Todhunter which turns her to suicide.

> "I cannot live. Richard despises me. I cannot bear
> the touch of my fingers or the sight of my face.
> Oh! I understand him now. He should not have
> kissed me so that last time. I wished to die while
> his mouth was on mine." (533)

This is the first entry in her diary after her marriage. Clare has enough self-hatred to accept Richard's condemnation of her. But she does not die of his bad opinion. She dies because in awakening her to her own sexuality Richard causes her to feel degraded by her marriage. She turns her physical revulsion toward her silly but harmless old husband against herself. Richard responds to Clare's marriage with the same physical morbidity with which he responds to his own seduction. Clare has no defense against his contempt since she has no ego-strength. That is, Clare's whole emotional life has been obedience to her mother and worship of Richard. She has no sense of self independent of their approval. The awakening of her sexuality which Richard's kiss inadvertently effects serves only to add force to her tremendous capacity for masochism.

Instead of fulfilling our expectation that the loyal love-sick girl wil be rewarded for her fanatical adoration of the hero, Meredith consciously jars us by violating the novelistic convention he has very carefully invoked. Clare's story poses a question we are unaccustomed to asking: What would become of Fanny or Agnes or Laura if they were allowed to totally renounce their sexuality and their selfhood as they all stand prepared to do? Meredith breaks apart the conventional expectations of the heroine by making clear that selfless infatuation for the wandering hero is in fact a form of self-hatred and is ultimately suicidal.

Clare's death foreshadows Lucy's death of "brain-fever" which Gillain Beer points out is "a recognizable stress illness, related to enforced passivity in emotonal crises," a stance too often expected of Victorian women.[22] Lucy's passive victimization is partly the result of Sir Austin's and Richard's brutal expectations of her.[23] But Lucy is not a mere victim anymore than Clare is. She enters the marriage from willful blindness of the consequences:

> Ah! why should she doubt that his great love was the first law to her? Why should she not believe that she would wreck him by resisting? And if she suffered, O sweet to think it was for his sake! Sweet to shut out Wisdom; accept total blindness, and be led by him. (309)

The heroine, unlike the hero, is by social necessity passive--but passivity is no less culpable than heroic aggression to Meredith's unvictorian mind. Lucy commits one of the central

---

[22] Beer, p. 14.

[23] As Richard leaves her to fight his duel, he tells her "You are brave, and you will bear it" despite her protestations that she knows now she cannot bear passive suffering with no cost to herself (585). Sir Austin pushes her past her capacities, thinking nothing is too much to ask "of _her_" especially for the sake of the new heir (569 and 588).

sins of the novel by closing her eyes to Wisdom[24] and becoming a "dutiful slave" to her lover; her willingness to suffer is no more admirable than Clare's and has the same result.

Like Richard, Lucy begins as a moral innocent. But she grows to be "the most inflexible little Heroine in the Three Kingdoms" when she usurps Mrs. Berry's wedding ring (347). More importantly she makes the fatal mistake of accepting Adrian's proposal that she feign cowardice to Richard so he will not know that it is his father who refuses to receive them together:

> Adrian looked in her face, as much to say: Now are you capable of this piece of heroism? And it did seem hard to her that she should have to tell Richard she shrank from any trial. But the proposition chimed in with her fears and her wishes: she thought the Wise Youth very wise: the poor child was not insensible to his flattery, and the subtler flattery of making herself in some measure a sacrifice to the home she had disturbed. She agreed to simulate as Adrian had suggested. (411)

The ruse is a terrible mistake because it destroys Richard's confidence in her and undermines his sense of the nobility of his elopement. His misguided decision is partly due to the cowardice, ignorance, small vanity, and trustingness of

---

[24]Sight is a central metaphor in the novel. Two of Sir Austin's characteristic stances are hiding himself from the penetrating glances of others (often behind a mask), and willfully blinding himself to his moral responsibilities. In contrast, Lady Blandish, "a dead shot with her eyes when she used them," gradually learns to see through the Baronet until we see the very end of the novel through her eyes. Hence,

the "poor child" who is very much alone in the world. But it is also the result of the "subtler flattery" of making herself a martyr to the Feverel pride, a piece of heroinism suited to her expectations of "sweet" suffering for her husband's sake.

Despite his sympathy with her suffering Meredith never applauds Lucy's propensity for martyrdom. She is as much the heroine as Richard is the hero--and as heroism is essentially destructive of others, so heroinism is self-destructive. When Richard seizes Lucy he is characterized as the Dick Turpin demanding "Happiness" of the world without expecting to have to pay for it (386). But when the "Heroine" has "risen to the measure of the hero" by seizing Mrs. Berry's ring, she exclaims "What it brings me I must bear" (349-350). She is as heroically ready to suffer exaggerated penalties as he is to expect no penalty at all.

Although Lucy learns through suffering to abandon her "heroic weakness" to some extent,[25] she is still only able to act positively in response to male guidance. That is, she does whatever Austin Wentworth and then Sir Austin tell her to do. She controls herself so violently in Richard's illness when Sir Austin asks her to keep away from her

---

Lucy's gesture of willfully closing her eyes to her responsibilities is an especially significant action.

[25] p. 341. See also pp. 569, 585, 588.

husband that she turns the justified anger she feels toward
Richard against herself. In her delirium we learn that she
feels that her husband has abandoned her to the flames which
are destroying her.[26] Although we are told when Lucy is
first presented that she has the faculty to "peruse the
sights of the earth," her dependent situation, her youth,
and most of all her heroism prevent her from ever using it
fully. Lucy's heroic death represents her failure as well
as Richard's to find a better way to live.

---

[26] The flames, of course, are meant to echo Richard's boyhood arson.

CHAPTER II

The Egoist and the New Woman

-1-

Between The Ordeal of Richard Feverel and The Egoist are twenty years, and six novels. Three of the novels, Sandra Belloni (1861), its sequel, Vittoria (1865), and Rhoda Fleming (1863), are significant steps toward The Egoist's presentation of the sexual politics of courtship. The heroines of these three novels are working class women with strong characters who are tested by male egoism. Sandra is an opera singer committed to the Manzini revolution. Rhoda is a farm girl who seeks to restore the reputation of her sister, Dahlia, who has been seduced by an upper-class young man. The central moral drama of these novels is the women's vulnerability to the duplicity and bullying of the men, and to the uncertainty of their own emotions.[1] Not

---

[1] Rhoda Fleming is about two very different sisters, Rhoda and Dahlia, both farm girls who attract the notice of rich city men. Dahlia is soft and passionate and ends by dying young, a ruined woman made saintly by the enormity of her suffering. Rhoda hates the name of love because of her sister's seduction. She is cold and calculating and, in the name of honor, cruelly forces her sister into a disastrous marriage. The sense/sensibility dichotomy is very exact and clearly Meredith is playing out some abstract scenario which doesn't quite come off. The same juxtaposition of the self-reliant woman and the victimized woman is certainly behind the characterization of Clara and Laetitia.

surprisingly, Sandra ends up a widow, Dahlia a solitary, ruined woman, for Meredith's "independent" women, as they were called, are primarily isolated and defenseless women. Sandra and Dahlia each attempt suicide. Yet they are clearly more in control of their lives than the truly suicidal Clare Doria or the martyred Lucy Feverel, and they prepare the way for Clara Middleton, who was hailed as the first "new woman" in English fiction.[2]

Sir Willoughby Patterne, the Egoist, was also a cultural emblem for more than a generation. In fact, the sexual politics implicit in his characterization are clearer than those in hers. Sir Willoughby owes a great deal to Sir Austin Feverel[3] and to Sir Austin's prototype, Dombey. But by making the tyrannical father into an inappropriately tenacious lover, Meredith created a rich comic character, less menacing, but intended to be more devastating to the reader. Sir Willoughby is meant to disturb the male reader, because he is a "pattern" of exploitative male sexuality. And in fact Robert Louis Stevenson was painfully convinced that he was himself the model, even after Meredith explained that Sir Willoughby was drawn from the sex as a whole.[4]

---

[2] Jack Lindsay, George Meredith: His Life and Work (London: Bodley Head, 1956), p. 240.

[3] In fact Meredith interrupted his work on The Egoist (1879) to revise Feverel for republication (1878).

[4] See Lionel Stevenson, The Ordeal of George Meredith:

At the same time, the simplicity of the comic target makes readers much more comfortable than the more complex mixture of sympathy and detestation which surrounds Sir Austin. The mood of the novel is much sunnier and better humored. Only in the short story "The Case of General Ople and Lady Camper" (1877)--significantly a tale of caricature used as a moral purgative--does Meredith also maintain such a sunny, simple tone. He himself was less comfortable with it than his modern readers. He compained while he was writing the novel that it was "a comedy, with only one half of me in it, unlikely therefore to take either the public or my friends."[5] And further

> as it comes mainly from the head and has nothing to kindle imagination, I thirsted to get rid of it soon after conception and it became a struggle in which health suffered. . . .[6]

Comic simplification offended Meredith's imagination, which was basically antipathetic to "patterns" of any kind. Meredith's intellect delighted in complexities, tensions, conflicts, and it was only by carefully withholding this energy that he could construct, as he did in this novel only, a plot as shapely and harmonious as that of <u>Tom Jones</u> or <u>Emma</u>.

<u>A Biography</u> (New York: Scribners, 1953), pp. 244-5. Hereafter referred to as "Stevenson."

[5] Stevenson, p. 221.

[6] <u>Letters</u>, Vol. II, 542.

Meredith's famous lecture on "Comedy and the Uses of the Comic Spirit" was delivered in 1877, and in formulating his ideas on comedy he turned to Moliere as virtually the sole model writer of true, wholesome comedy. The main thesis of the lecture is echoed in the far less lucid preface to The Egoist. Certainly he thought of this novel as an application of his theory of comedy. In the lecture Meredith says that true comedy should provoke "thoughtful laughter" which will purge folly through self-awareness. The key to the social function of Meredithian comedy is in his precept that it is the "first condition of sanity to believe" that "our civilization is founded in common-sense" and that comedy appeals to that common-sense and is therefore the handmaiden of civilization.[7] It is the province of the Comic Spirit to reform manners and morals through the sympathetic ridicule of the uncommonsensical. Sir Willoughby is accordingly shaped as a new comic type to set beside the miser and the misanthrope, presumably a creative process which required too much head and too little imagination.

It is not hard to see the basic formula-writing which Meredith may have been complaining of in the comments quoted above. Here is Willoughby's response to Laetitia's refusal

---

[7] Essay on the Idea of Comedy and the Uses of the Comic Spirit, Volume 7 of the standard edition, The Works of George Meredith. Memorial Edition, 29 vols. (London: Constable & Co., 1915). See pp. 88-89.

of his hand in marriage, a refusal which occurs after ten years of unrequited love for him have exhausted her:

> You loved me. You are silent? But you confessed it. Then you confess it was a love that could die! Are you unable to perceive how that redounds to my discredit? In other words, you charge me with incapacity to sustain a woman's love. You accuse me of inspiring a miserable passion that cannot last a lifetime.[8]

Even as formula comedy, this is quite fine. But in fact there is more to Sir Willoughby than "a leg" and Egoism. Not only do we get farther inside of him than we would if Meredith were really Moliere, we also see him from Clara's perspective.

And from Clara's perspective, he is a formidable adversary. While we laugh at him, we do not overlook her shrinking before him. This double vision of the Egoist is a physical reality in the novel. It begins with the wonderful scene of Clara's arrival at Patterne Hall in Chapter VII, when she is first aware of her sexual revulsion for her lover. Here is the scene:

> . . . Sir Willougby led her on his arm across the threshold, whispering "Soon for good!" In reply to the whisper, she begged for more of the story of young Crossjay who had made an explosion in Willoughby's laboratory "Come into the laboratory," said he, a little less laughingly than softly, and Clara begged her father to come and see young Crossjay's latest pranks. Sir Willoughby whispered to her of the length of their separation and his joy to welcome her to the

---

[8] p. 489. All citations are to the standard edition of the Works, Volume 6.

> house where she would reign as mistress _very_ soon.
> He numbered the weeks. He whispered, "Come." In
> the hurry of the moment she did not examine a light-
> ning terror that shot through her. It passed, and
> was no more than the shadow which bends the summer
> grasses, leaving a ruffle of her ideas in wonder of
> her having feared herself for something. Her father
> was with them. She and Willoughby were not yet alone.

Sir Willoughby leads them into the library, where Dr. Middleton becomes engrossed in Vernon Whitford's scholarly notes.

> She was led to think that Willoughby had drawn them
> to the library with the design to be rid of her pro-
> tector, and she began to fear him. She proposed to
> pay her respects to the ladies Eleanor and Isabel.
> They were not to be seen, and a footman reported in
> the drawing-room that they were out driving. She
> grasped young Crossjay's hand. Sir Willoughby dis-
> patched him to Mrs. Montague, the housekeeper, for
> a tea of cakes and jam.
>   "Off!" he said, and the boy had to run.
>   Clara saw herself without a shield.
>   "And the garden!" she cried. "I love the garden.
> I must go and see what flowers are up with you. In
> spring I care most for wild-flowers, and if you will
> show me daffodils, and crocuses, and anemones--"
>   "My dearest Clara! My Bride!" said he.
>   "Because they are vulgar flowers?" she asked him
> artlessly, to account for his detaining her.

This is adroitly written comedy of manners. The chase from room to room is not physical but verbal and works upon a pretense of misunderstanding; Clara ignores Willoughby's cues that he wants to kiss her, Willoughby ignores her obvious attempts to stop him. On one level a conversation about Crossjay, beneath it a battle of wits, the whole forming a graceful skirmish over a kiss.

The maneuvers for privacy and protection are stagy, as is Sir Willoughby's precious lover's speech ("You are mine, my Clara--utterly mine, every thought, every feeling. We are one; the world may do its worst," etc.). But we also feel the weight of Clara's oppression, which lies outside of the comedy of manners mode:

> She came out of his embrace with the sensations of the frightened child that has had its dip in sea-water, sharpened to think that after all it was not so severe a trial. Such was her idea, and she said to herself immediately, "What am I that I should complain?" Two minutes earlier she would not have thought it, but humiliated pride falls lower than humbleness.

Clara's "pride" was her foolish belief that she could assert herself against her lover's wishes. Willoughby's kiss has taught her her real powerlessness; he has put her in her place.

> She did not blame him; she fell in her own esteem, less because she was the betrothed Clara Middleton, which was now palpable as a shot in the breast of a bird, than that she was a captured woman, of whom it is absolutely expected that she must submit, and when she would rather be gazing at flowers. Clara had the shame of her sex. They cannot take a step without becoming a bondswoman--into what a slavery!

Up to this point, as I have said, we have been watching a verbal rather than a physical struggle, although Clara has indeed been running from room to room to avoid being alone with Willoughby. The comedy of "artless" references to flowers, which are really artful evasions, ends with the kiss. Clara has not only lost the verbal skirmish, she has discovered with painful vividness ("a shot in the breast of a bird") that her body is no longer her own. The "shame of her sex" is like the shame of the ghetto, she thinks less of herself because she can be treated as a slave.

With a sure sense of control, Meredith now turns his attention to Willoughby, who not only mistakes Clara's coldness for prudishness, but he also delights in such a response!

> Sir Willoughby was enraptured with her. Even so purely, coldly, statue-like, Dian-like, would he have prescribed his bride's reception of his caress. The suffusion of crimson coming over her subsequently, showing her divinely feminine in reflective bashfulness, agreed with his highest definitions of female character.[9]

Clara's very disgust for him makes her more desirable to her lover. We are certainly laughing at Willoughby here, with his absurd Victorian demand for a statue-wife. But the parallel presentation makes us conscious that his "divinely feminine" bashfulness is her deep humiliation at "the shame of her sex," her "fall" in self-esteem raises her to meet his "highest definitions of female character." Meredith is using the conventional comic misunderstandings of comedy of manners as a vehicle for presenting the radically different worlds of men and women. Millamant and Mirabell are no longer speaking the same language.

We never lose sight of the fact that Sir Willoughby's narcissistic isolation makes a real prison for Clara. She is as much Clarissa (as her name implies) as she is Millamant.

---

[9] pp. 66-69.

She is cut off from the rest of the world in a "horrible isolation of secrecy" (144), for she is presumed to be happy with a perfect lover. She is "in the desert and alone" (142), confined to a dungeon, "and, oh terror, not . . . a quiet dungeon; the barren walls closed round her, talked, called for ardour, expected admiration" (111). Clara's predicament is a new one in English literature. She is engaged to a seemingly unobjectionable man. She is isolated by her revulsion from the prize of the neighborhood, and she must struggle to articulate the grounds of her distaste.

Meredith walks a thin line in keeping us amused with Willoughby, and yet letting us see Clara's increasing desperation. One reason why we do not get bored with Willoughby ourselves, is that in scenes that are at first glance strictly set pieces, displays of egoism, we are not only watching Willoughby. We are also watching Clara's mind come to grips with his character. For example, here is Willoughby complaining about Vernon's attempt to be self-supporting:

> "I want him here, and supposing he goes, he offends me; he loses a friend, and it will not be the first time that a friend has tried me too far; but if he offends me, he is extinct."
> "Is what?" cried Clara, with a look of fright.
> "He becomes to me as if he had never been. He is extinct."
> "In spite of your affection?"
> "On account of it, I might say. Our nature is mysterious, and mine as much so as any. Whatever my regrets, he goes out. This is not a language I talk to the world. I do the man no harm; I am not to be named unchristian. But--"
> Sir Willoughby mildly shrugged and indicated a

spreading wave of the arms.
"But do, do talk to me as you talk to the world, Willoughby; give me some relief" (105-6).

Again we have sure formula comedy: the man who thinks of his friends as reflections of his own goodness and power will consider them dead when they are no longer happy in heaven. Willoughby can see only one impediment to Vernon's extinction: his own regrets. By this time Willoughby's diction is itself a pat joke for the reader. Clara's questions lead him on to greater absurdities. But the absurdities increase her desperation as her vague fears turn to certain knowledge of his character.

Clara's keen sense of "dragging a log," of being "fixed in the mouth of a mine . . . chilled in subterranean sunlessness . . . with only the mystery of inefficient tallow-light in those caverns of the complacent talking man" (65), produces a tremendous languor in her:

> Liberty wore the aspect of a towering prison-wall. The desperate undertaking of climbing one side and dropping to the other was more than she, unaided could resolve on; consequently, as no one cared for her, a worthless creature might as well cease dreaming and stipulating for the fulfillment of her dreams; she might as well yield to her fate, nay, make the best of it. (144)

Her predicament begins to look like her fate. Her total powerlessness, the destruction of her self-esteem, and her isolation make this extraordinarily athletic and quick-witted girl hope to adjust to Willoughby. Her lover further destroys her sense of personal effectiveness by consistently ignoring her. He persists in seeing her as a "little brain" as well as "essentially feminine, that is, a parasite and a chalice" (50). If she is clever, he refuses to see it. For example, here the argument is their basic one over his affected misanthropy:

> "Two that love must have their substance in isolation."
> "No, they will be eating themselves up."
> "The purer the beauty, the more it will be out of the world."
> "But not opposed."
> "Put it this way," Willoughby condescended. "Has experience the same opinion of the world as ignorance?"
> "It should have more charity."
> "Does virtue feel at home in the world?"
> "Then, are you in favour of monasteries?"
> He poured a little runlet of half-laughter over her head of the sound assumed by genial compassion.
> It is irritating to hear that when we imagine we have spoken to the point. (75)

Clara is grateful to Vernon Whitford because he listens to what she says. He helps to restore her sense of her own existence and she is pleased "to hear Clara Middleton talked of and of her having been thought of" (139). Sir Willoughby's "attentions" to Clara take the form of empty compliments which delight him and exhaust her.

> "It seems to me that our minds are opposed."
> "I should," said he "have been awake to it at a single indication, be sure."
> "But I know," she pursued, "I have learnt, that the ideal of conduct for women is to subject their minds to the part of an accompaniment."
> "For women, my love?" My wife will be in natural harmony with me."
> "Ah!" She compressed her lips. The yawn would come. "I am sleepier here than anywhere."
> "Ours, my Clara, is the finest air of the kingdom. It has the effect of sea air."

> "But if I am always asleep here?"
> "We shall have to make a public exhibition of the beauty."
> This dash of his liveliness defeated her. (119)

Clara's yawns are the real toll of the Egoist. She yawns from boredom and complete demoralization. Her intelligence, her vitality, her spurts of combativeness, have so little effect on the world around her that she is defeated by her own strength. She is living in limbo:

> "And if I marry, and then--where will honour be then? I marry him to be true to my word of honour, and if then---" An intolerable languor caused her to sigh profoundly. It is written as she thought it; she thought in blanks, as girls do and some women. A shadow of the male Egoist is in the chamber of their brains overawing them. (133)

By desiring and treating Clara as if she were "the common male Egoist ideal of a waxwork sex," Willoughby robs her of her vitality. Significantly, he gives her her only weapon when he urges her to beware of marrying an Egoist.[10] Clara finds courage in the conceptualization of Egoism. When she finds the word for Willoughby, the clarity of her mind helps her to overcome the shadow of his tyrannical condescension.

-2-

It should be apparent that Clara is part of a large family of sisters which includes, for example, Millamant, Clarissa, and Emma. Perhaps we had best pause here and

---

[10] p. 115 and pp. 120-121.

consider what the comedy of manners mode signifies as a way of organizing human experience. Congreve, Richardson, Austen, Meredith: these are the names of some of the major practitioners of the comedy of manners in English. For all of them we can say that their literary worlds are construed as surface and depths. On the surface, wit, grace, elegance, sublety. Beneath, selfishness, lust, greed, vulgarity. This is what the comedy of manners says about the world: we are civilized, but civilization is fragile. Decorum, delicacy, manners, proprieties are tremendously important in the comedy of manners world, but they are so because passion and violence are always threatening to intrude and break the social order. This is what these four fictive worlds, for all their obvious diversity, hold in common. It is important to see Meredith's vision as a variant of this world.

It is easy to see how <u>The Egoist</u> could have been written as <u>The Way of the World</u>. Clara and Vernon, the true lovers, could unite to outwit the stiff and monied Sir Willoughby and the foolish Dr. Middleton. The quadrangular possibilities of Clara and Willoughby and Laetitia and Vernon are stock comedy of manners material. The comic <u>deus ex machina</u> of Crossjay under a coverlet is also out of the Restoration mode, and, as I have noted above, the novel is arranged, especially after Clara's crucial return from the railway station, as a series of staged scenes. Certainly the

brilliant finale, with Willoughby pretending to be engaged
to two different women at once is, one could almost say, the
finest bit of Restoration Comedy ever written. One would
not need to add any more witty dialogue, trickiness, or
characters at cross-purposes (remember, there is also Col.
De Craye!), but only to exaggerate into flatness the characters and situations we already have in order to have
Congreve's <u>Egoist</u>. The power plays are the same for Meredith
and Congreve. In each we enjoy the adroitness with which the
characters attack and counterattack without raising their
voices.

The resemblance to <u>Clarissa</u> is more subtle. Aside from
the obvious similarities in plot, the important thing that
Meredith took from Richardson is the thing that never happens.
That is, in both novels the social conventions in which the
heroines live prevent them from even having an honest conversation with their captors. Clarissa must be raped before
she can face Lovelace without her own delicacy prohibiting
her from directly speaking of her situation. She can never
demand that he marry her. Similarly, Willoughby subdues
Clara not by physical force but by verbal evasions, refusals
to understand her, which her own sense of decency prevents
her from combatting. In the scene of the kiss for example,
Willoughby exploits the fact that Clara, as a Victorian woman,
cannot explicitly refer to his kissing her, even to deny it.

It is the same mechanism which keeps Clarissa imprisoned in a brothel. One of the most painful aspects of The Egoist is that Clara can never have it out with Willoughby and her father. Her prison is partially formed by the decorums of her society.

Jane Austen occupies a special place in this line of practitioners of the comedy of manners. Social gesture acquires a special resonance in her novels for in her fictional universe manners are morals. How one behaves socially, how one follows the rules of society--the simple rules of politeness--is indicative of what one is. When we watch a Restoration play we are delighted by the cleverness with which manners can conceal real motives and passions. The scenes between Clarissa and Lovelace partake of some of this same pleasure. But in Jane Austen we find the opposite pleasure, we are delighted by what is revealed by small details. Mr. Elton's slightly sugared politeness marks him as a snob, a hypocrite. Emma's tactlessness to Miss Bates is the crucial betrayal of her vanity and selfishness. Small social gestures become enormous moral acts. No one has to be raped in Austen's world for us to feel the presence of real brutality (in fact a brutality much more convincing than Richardson's melodramatic physical violence) in the way people treat each other in their daily lives.

Like Austen, Meredith is fascinated with the signifi-

cance of slight gestures, with "making out" (to use the
Jamesian phrase for this effort) the underlying moral truths
for which manners are a sort of symbolic language. Neither
Meredith nor James could have written with the attention they
give to the momentary details of social intercourse if it
had not been for Austen; but it is in her novels alone that
goodness is directly represented as good manners. Jane
Austen sets the social comedy of Congreve upon the firm basis
of a society which is indeed "founded in common-sense" as
Meredith liked to believe it was. Meredith almost desper-
ately clings to the Austen dispensation. He rests his theory
of comedy upon it. But in fact he perceives a much more
destructive society.

Jane Austen was untouched by the American and French
Revolutions and the Napoleonic Wars. Meredith was stirred
deeply and forever by the internationalism of his Moravian
schooling and by the continental rebellions and the final
Chartist agitation of 1848-9. The prospect of another, saner,
more humane world order was an abiding belief for him.[11]
He tried to reconcile it with his belief in the achievement
of the existing social organization by a vague faith in a
society evolving by natural law. Although he detested the

---

[11] For Meredith's political passions see Jack Lindsay's marxist biography, <u>George Meredith</u> (London: Bodley Head, 1956) and the more realistic appraisal in Norman Kelvin <u>A Troubled Eden: Nature and Society in the Works of George Meredith</u>

scientific and technological emphasis of Victorian progressivism, his radicalism (he called himself a Radical) was another form of the same faith. Like other Victorian Radicals, he barely knew of Marx and had only the vaguest notion of a different economic ordering. His politics were eccentric and inconsistent,[12] although he was certainly always political.

So Meredith had neither Jane Austen's trust in the justice of social life nor the true radical's vision of the essential corruption of the existing order. He had instead vaguely conceived though often passionate leftist politics combined with a very English respect for order, all complicated by his deep personal shame over his own lower middle class origins. Luckily for him and for us--for it is the driving intellectual force behind his novels--Meredith had a mind which delighted in tension and complexity. He came to terms with his political ambivalence the same way he came to terms with his shame and guilt over his first marriage. He learned to regard the acceptance of evil in society, in ourselves, and in those we love, as the primary moral response to the world. Hence his reiterated condemnation of stances

---

(Stanford: 1961), especially Chapter 2, "Society is a Battleground."

[12] For example, Lindsay has a great deal of trouble with Meredith's support of British imperialist ventures. Furthermore, while writing Vittoria and Beauchamp's Career, both novels which espouse Radical politics, he was doing Tory hack work.

he saw as simplistic denials of the mixture of good and evil
in the world: misanthropy, cynicism, sentimentality, and
christianity are obsessive targets of his on these grounds.
There have been many attempts to work Meredith's pronounce-
ments on nature and society into a coherent whole. But
there is not an intellectual coherence but an imaginative
coherence to his perception of the world as a social comedy,
based not on a just society represented in a code of manners,
but upon a perfectible nature which operates by conflict.

Despite its vagueness, Meredith's world-view is impres-
sive in its opposition to the more usual western view of the
moral universe as a pyramid whose apex is reason (or ego)
but whose bulk is appetite (or id). For Meredith had his
own version of the platonic/freudian triad, but it is significantly non-hierarchic. For Meredith, blood, brain, and
spirit must be in harmony for the individual or the society
to be healty.[13] And each member of the triad is both good
and evil. Meredith does not fear disruptions of the blood

---

[13] The crucial statement of this theme comes in "The Woods
of Westermain" in these unfortunately jarring lines:
>   Each of us in sequent birth,
>   Blood and brain and spirit, three
>   (say the deepest gnomes of Earth)
>   Join for true felicity.
>   Are they parted, then expect
>   Someone sailing will be wrecked:
>   Separate hunting are they sped,
>   Scan the morsel coveted.
>   Earth that Triad is: she hides
>   Joy from him who that divides;

more than the false mastery of the brain. Similarly, he does not see civilization as the precarious lid on the boiling cauldron of primitivism (a vision of the social world which is, as I said above, a starting point for the comedy of manners as Congreve's example makes quite clear.) Here, for example, Clara is fighting both a social and a natural force:

> The Egoist is our fountain head, primeval man; the primitive is born again, the elemental reconstituted. Born again into new conditions, the primitive may be highly polished of men and forfeit nothing save the roughness of his original nature. He is not only his own father; he is ours, and he is also our son. We have produced him, he us. . . . Degenerate or not (and there is no reason to suppose it) Sir Willoughby was a social Egoist, fiercely imaginative in whatsoever concerned him. He had discovered a greater realm than that of the sensual appetites, and he rushed across and around it in his conquering period with an Alexander's pride. (476-477)

Meredith rejects the proposal that the primitive is a degeneration of the civilized: "We have produced him, he us." This is a significant advance over the theory of society founded in simple English common sense which he advances in the "Essay on Comedy." Here socialization has only discovered a "greater realm" of pleasures to the savage. Lust turns to voluptuousness and the desire for possession. Mere-

---

        Showers it when three are one,
        Glassing her in unison.
See Joseph Priestley's discussion of this issue in <u>George Meredith</u> (1926), Chapter III, and also Kelvin, Chapter 4, which compares Meredith's notions of struggle and natural beneficence with those of other Victorians.

dith sees the sexual politics of chastity in women quite clearly; he associates it consistently with the harem.

Civilization, which teaches men to see the submissive chaste bride and to value her purity, is here quite vividly described in terms of the jungle:

> Jealousy of a woman is the primitive egoism seeking to refine in a blood gone to savagery under apprehension of an invasion of rights; it is in action the tiger threatened by a rifle when his paw is rigid on quick flesh; he tears the flesh for rage at the intruder. The Egoist, who is our original male in giant form, has no bleeding victim beneath his paw, but there was the sex to mangle. Much as he prefers the well-behaved among women, who can worship and fawn and in whom terror can be inspried, in his wrath he could make of Beatrice a Lesbia Quadrantaaria. (277)

Meredith clearly sees that the decorums of society which impose female chastity are only expressions of the "original male." Common sense is clearly no true guide to this civilization.

Meredith is able to hold these two opposing views of society--as graceful order founded in common sense, and as a recomposition in a new key of the life of the jungle--by taking the faith he wanted to put into the social order and transferring it to a vaguely (he would say "philosophically") perceived natural order. Society may be corrupt, but it should not be utterly violated because it is slowly evolving by natural processes, and most of all by conflict, into a higher and saner order. He can have it both ways. Order is good, and conflict is not threatening.

The victory of Meredith's imagination in accepting conflict and guilt is most easily grasped by comparing him to other Victorian novelists. Thackeray, for example, came of a similar background--pretensions to gentility tempered by financial strain. Both men suffered in childhood from the absence of their mothers, and in adulthood from disastrous marriages which left them with many guilty regrets. Thackeray associated his wife's madness with his pursuit of his career. To think of the mawkish sentimentality of Thackeray's domestic scenes, the impotence of his good men, the constant association of goodness with victimization, is to see how a first-rate imagination can be fettered by misfortune. Like Meredith, Thackeray was fascinated and repelled by the new capitalist managerial class, but unlike Meredith he rushes into a domestic, passive religiousity as the only salvation from the competitive, aggressive life. Thackeray's imagination is limited by his escapist rush to a sheltered "feminine" innocence. Meredith was able to transfer his religious faith, despite his despair at the social order, onto a complex nature. He sought neither fierce competition-- the security of playing well according to the way of the world--nor the resignation from the game which was so common to the Victorian spirit. He sought the courage to face a sometimes frightening, sometimes conforting world. One in no way demeans Thackeray by admiring Meredith's courage.

But reading Thackeray's terrible fear of life between the lines of <u>Vanity Fair</u> can help us to appreciate the achievement of Meredith's imaginative victory over despair.

Unlike other Victorian novelists, Meredith's emotional center is not in a passive, victimized, close domestic life, but in a complex nature which reflects both the aggressiveness Thackeray and Dickens associated with men and the world of business, and the comfort they associated with good women. Near the end of his life, Meredith remarked "Life is combative, necessarily so. Let us be combative, but let us also be kind."[14] His personal ethic is close to his aesthetic. He looked to the social comedy of his novels to express the combativeness of life, especially the combat between men and women. Aside from the question of the overall success of these novels we can admire the integrity of spirit which sought to realize in fiction this struggle to be effective and to be humane.

-3-

Because of his real lack of faith in the common-sense foundation of his society, Meredith necessarily found it difficult to write "mainly from the head" after his own rules of comedy. He lacked Congreve's facile morality and

---

[14] <u>Letters</u>, Vol. III, 798.

Jane Austen's conservatism, yet he was drawn to their mode
because of his deep awareness of the significance of social
gesture. In imitation of them and of Molière, he sets up a
recipe for comedy which works well for Sir Willoughby and
brilliantly in some key dramatic scenes. One thinks in
particular of the ending of the novel and especially of the
three scenes of social maneuvering which are wonderfully
funny: the confrontation in the library in which Clara and
Willoughby alternately coax Dr. Middleton in and out of the
room; Vernon's intimation to Willoughby that he knows of his
proposal to Laetitia; and, of course, the scene of "Willoughby's generalship" in which he plays Mr. Dale and Dr. Middleton off against each other before the eyes of his gossiping
neighbors, holding them both as potential fathers-in-law
until the last possible moment. But it is easy to see why
Meredith was strained in writing thus, for while his head
works on the social complications, his imagination is stirred
by the claustrophobia of the drawingroom. The middle scene
of the comic trio I just mentioned is figuratively played
under the star of Iphigenia, Clara's unconscious emblem for
her father's willingness to sacrifice her.[15] She comes
perilously close to the knife, and is only extricated by
comic chance.

---

[15] See p. 539, and pp. 547-8.

The comedy and the confinement of the novel are interdependent. Clara is forced into the world of comedy of manners fencing because she has no other way out of the engagement. In speaking of the decline in birching boys (one of Meredith's hobby horses) Dr. Middleton remarks, "This growing too fine is our way of relapsing upon barbarism" (537). The remark is made in the midst of the final comic mix-up, and of course refers as well to the barbarism masked by decorum which is Clara's Ordeal. In her last moment of struggle Clara is pledged to one hour and to the space of Willoughby's grounds. She is locked into the drawingroom comedy. And so are we.

It is hard for the modern reader to see why Clara does not simply run away. Perhaps the most troublesome part of the novel is her abortive flight to London. Like Richard's elopement and Diana's attempted elopement, it is the turning point in the novel. All our sympathies are with her as she rushes away from the humiliation and imprisonment of Willoughby's house. She has asked straight-forwardedly for a release from her engagement, and Willoughby has taken the only "gentlemanly" way out. He pretends not to understand her. Then he traps her father with his family wine.

Running seems her only alternative. The reasons for her return are vague. At first, she is not at all moved by Vernon's quiet reminder of her duty to her father and to

the man she is pledged to marry. De Craye actively encourages
her to run, and it seems to be his vulgarity which tips the
scales for her. But this is something we can only infer.
There is no moment of decision. She returns not as the
result of a conscious decision, but in a fit of overwhelming
languor.

> Both in thought and sensation she was like a flower
> beaten to earth, and thanked her feminine mask for
> not showing how nerveless and languid she was. She
> could have accused Vernon of a treacherous cunning
> for imposing it on her free will to decide her fate.(338

She comes back without any prospect of winning her freedom
by her own efforts (and in fact it takes Crossjay, De Craye,
Vernon, and Willoughby himself to finally extricate her,
while she can do nothing but stall and beg for time). She
comes back though "her whole heart was for flight" (334).
But by the logic of the plot (which does extricate her) and
by our reliance upon Vernon as the moral spokesman for the
author, we are to take Clara's languid return as a morally
responsible gesture, an act which somehow affirms Vernon's
dictum that "there is no freedom for the weak" (338).

It would seem that to the contrary, freedom was waiting
on the railway car, and only weakness sends her back to
Willoughby and her father. Of course we must recognize that
Clara is a nineteenth century woman and is therefore doing
something quite scandalous in leaving the "protection"
(as it would be thought) of her fiancé and her father. The

presence of De Craye makes this clear. In fact, Clara is not running off to get a job or live in lodgings. She is running away in order to create a scandal, because she knows that scandal is the only weapon she has against Willoughby. It is not the running which is effective, but the wildness it represents. Jack Lindsay rightly reminds us that Dr. Middleton's term for Clara's act is "jacobist," i.e. revolutionary.[16]

Why isn't the novel on the side of the revolution? It is an important question, given the claustrophobia of the society it represents. Why doesn't Clara challenge the social order and get on the train?

The historical answer is only partly satisfactory, given Meredith's clear disgust for the dependency of women upon which the social restrictions are based. I think that in order to understand why Clara decides as she does--and in fact why the choice is presented to her--we must recognize that Clara has a lot of fictional predecessors at that railroad station. It is almost a staple of the English novel that one must be capable of renunciation before one is worthy of reward, particularly in love. The proposal scene in *Emma* is a paradigm of the pattern, and indeed Meredith echoes it in Clara's and Vernon's mutual silence on Willough-

---

[16]Lindsay, p. 240.

by's plan to marry them. Mr. B. must renounce Pamela (and Pamela must renounce the freedom she has been fighting for for 300 pages), Ann Elliot renounces Wentworth, Wentworth renounces Ann, Jane Eyre must renounce Rochester (and after his mutilation, he must renounce her), Maggie Tolliver renounces both Philip and Stephen, Dobbin renounces Amelia, Agnes renounces David Copperfield, and, of course, the convention reaches its height in the fiction of Henry James, where there are finally more renunciations than consummations. The period of trial, the proof of selfishness, the denial of lust or love, seem to be part of the mythic structure of bourgeois courtship. It has its ancestors, no doubt, in the courtly love tradition, but why does it reappear so strongly and persistently not as a denial of adultery, but as a denial of happiness itself? Why must all of these characters prove their worthiness by varying degrees of self-immolation?

It would seem that that is what the society demands. Thackeray's mistrust of success is the rule rather than the aberration. In English fiction though novels usually end on the marriage bed. There is the persistent refrain that discipline not desire is the road to happiness. In each situation, of course, the reasons for the renunciation are clear. But the question remains--why do such situations recur? Why is it abstinence which makes the heart grow fonder and the soul grow stronger?

Meredith is arguing two ways. Social decorum is destructive, yet inviolable. Clara is locked into the drawingroom, forced to dance the lions' minuet, and yet we are told that it would be cowardly of her to run. Her languid return is a courageous reentry into the social battle. The dance may be deadly, but you cannot get on the train, because fulfillment of desire, the direct grasping of happiness, is a social danger. The marriage of young lovers reaffirms and sustains the values of the community, yet at the same time it would seem that the love of young lovers threatens the social structure. Love is over and over again associated not with fulfilled desires but with self-discipline. One's lover is often, like Vernon or Mr. Knightley, one's moral guide, and so love itself instructs the lover in the virtues of social restraint. Pamela and Jane Eyre perform this role for their lovers, but it is more often the man who is the active chastening influence. Women--like Tom Jones' Sophia and David Copperfield's Agnes--are the reward for rather than the model of moral growth. In both these cases the heroes must learn, like Clara, not to seek immediate gratification, but to conform to bourgeois decorum and to accept the bourgeois values of moderation and domesticity before they can win the hand of the redeeming beauty.

So Clara cannot get on that train, but Meredith is right in making her decision the result of languid acquiescence in the prison code, rather than the result of reasoned moral choice. Male egoism and the refined barbarism of society have the same effect upon her. Despite his attempt to attribute Clara's decision to Vernon Whitford's knightleyism, Meredith's surer sense of psychology makes him portray the return more truthfully as the effect of powerlessness.

-4-

One of the major difficulties with the train scene is Vernon himself. Vernon and Laetitia, like most secondary Meredith characters, bear examination in their own right. For me, the novel is most successful as a story about Clara and Willoughby, and least successful in its treatment of Vernon and Laetitia, although the ways in which it fails here are extremely interesting, both aesthetically and as a barometer of sexual politics in 1879.

Of course, Vernon is a portrait of Meredith's dear friend Leslie Stephen. It is extraordinary to have two such conflicting portraits of the same man as this upright, earnest, gentle young man and the oppressive Mr. Ramsay in To The Lighthouse. Certainly a man is a different person to his daughter and to his friends, but it is hard to understand how Meredith could have been completely blind to the male egoism so central to Virginia Woolf's portrait of her father. It is especially odd since Mr. Ramsay's particularly characteristic destructive trick of manipulating women by the force of his unhappiness appears first in English fiction as Sir Willoughby's conscious attempts at pathos. Had we no knowledge of Leslie Stephen we might recognize Sir Willoughby as the prototype of the self-pitying, self-dramatizing Mr. Ramsay. Yet Meredith actually took the young Mr. Ramsay as the model for the Egoist's nemesis, Vernon Whitford.

Perhaps Meredith did see Leslie's uglier side, as he said he saw the Egoist in all men; perhaps Sir Willoughby as well as Vernon owes something to Leslie Stephen. It is impossible to know. But from all his letters to Leslie and Julia Stephen we must conclude that Meredith loved and respected his friend for precisely the same brand of intellectual earnestness and physical exertion he gives to Vernon. It is also apparent from the letters that Meredith respected the quality of the Stephens' marriage. We have a letter to "Mrs. Leslie" in which he chides her for publicly opposing women's suffrage, although he is clearly charmed and delighted by her feeling that the vote of "her Leslie" was sufficient.[17] After Leslie's death in 1904 he wrote to Vanessa Stephen:

> One of the most beloved of my friends has gone from sight, and though I feel that he remains with me and has his lasting place in our literature, this day's news darkens my mind. Last Autumn I was near to

---

[17]*Letters*, Vol. II, 261.

>going. The loss of my friend spurs the wish that
>I had preceded him. He was the one man in my
>knowledge worthy of being mated with your mother.
>I could say no more of any man's nobility.[18]

Leslie Stephen did not marry Julia Duckworth until May 26, 1878, when Meredith was well into his novel, but the sense of a "noble" man worthy of mating with a superior woman describes Meredith's sense of Vernon and Clara as well as of Leslie and Julia. It is significant that the real marriage appears in <u>To the Lighthouse</u> as the very type of the old order, though Meredith can see Leslie as the worthy mate for his Clara.

This selective vision of reality is not surprising when we remember Meredith's own marital history. He quickly abandonded witty verbal women after the disastrous battling with Mary Peacock Nicolls. His second wife he referred to as a "mud-fort" for her ability to absorb verbal "broadsides" without response.[19] He saved his wit for flirtations with lively younger women like Janet Ross. He was not so fond of sexual equality that he actually wanted to live with it.

It is good to keep these confusions in mind because they may help to explain the singular lack of energy and vitality in the characterization of Vernon. Vernon has identifiable,

---

[18]<u>Letters</u>, Vol. III, 1491.

[19]Stevenson, 185.

coherent traits--he is industrious, fair, a champion of underdogs and small boys, truthful, scrupulously honorable (with an emphasis on the scruples), an admirable swimmer and walker, and he sleeps under a beautiful cherry tree. But unlike the other characters in the novel--Clara, Willoughby, and even Laetitia--Vernon has no believable vital center of being. We hardly feel his presence, except as pallid stolidity. At one point we are told that his blood is secretly "chasing wild with laughter" but it is not an easy thing to believe of him (540).

Though not a fully realized emotional presence in the novel, Vernon might still have been a compelling moral presence. But as we have seen, Vernon is oddly inadequate to this role as well. The plot clearly calls for him to be Mr. Knightley--someone who is undebatably correct, but also graceful and forceful. Mr. Knightley's goodness always takes the form of the graceful and competent gesture--sending his coach for Miss Bates, asking Harriet to dance. This is the kind of moral presence the comedy of manners format of The Egoist is calling for. But instead of Mr. Knightley's generoisty of spirit, we have Vernon's tightness. His virtue consists chiefly in holding himself back, watching Clara fight off Willoughby's suffocating grip, while maintaining the proper English novel pose of renunciation. Vernon is graceless and largely impotent. It is, after all, the comic chance of Crossjay's seclusion which rescues Clara.

Kate Millett has complained that Meredith confused the sexual revolution with a marriage market by handing Clara over to Vernon at the end of the novel.[20] I think it is ahistorical to expect a happy ending with an unmarried heroine in 1879, but it is still very true that Vernon is no answer to the problem. I doubt that Millett would share my willingness to accept Mr. Knightley (who is indeed a very dangerous woman's fantasy hero) as a replacement, but it is certainly true that he would dispel some of the uneasiness which Vernon provokes. But Mr. Knightley is impossible in 1879. Not only is he rich and feudal (no longer a possible model for goodness), he is effective. The Victorian association of power with corruption, innocence with weakness, is part of what emasculates Vernon. He is going off to London to struggle for success with his pen, certainly staunch and brave and (what is more than Dickens and Thackeray could have imagined) political. But there is no imaginative energy in him. Vernon is not wholly present, either as fantasy (as is Mr. Knightley), or as psychological reality (as is Willoughby).

The Egoist marks a point in cultural history where

---

[20] Sexual Politics (New York: 1969), p. 139.

heroes are losing energy and heroines are gaining it. Clara is indeed the New Woman in the exhilaration she brings to the world. Vernon's emancipation from Willoughby has none of that exhilaration. Dickens' heroes could go and get a job in the colonies. Meredith cannot find an economic or a moral base for Vernon, and so his life-affirming speeches are empty. His life is full of the burden of uncertain work and grim responsibility. Mr. Knightley, also a great walker, moves gracefully along with the weight of responsibility upon his shoulders. Seventy years later, Vernon is strenuously hiking up the Alps with the weight of the world on his back.

Laetitia is also a pale and energyless character. She works most successfully in the novel as a plot device, an instrument of retribution. A faded beauty and failed poet, the victim of Sir Willoughby's emotional exploitation, Laetitia ends up the representatively exploitative woman, marrying without love for money and power. It is a fitting reversal of the sexual politics of the situation. It is also fitting that Sir Willoughby who has prized Laetitia as a mirror in whose eyes he can seek out and embrace his own inflated reflection (29-30), ends up with a Laetitia whose "hard detective eye" will be a scourge and a curb (618-9). Laetitia's own motives are also appropriate, for the novel makes clear throughout that her passivity, and in fact her very infatuation are the direct result of her economic dependency.

Another strong element in the characterization of Laetitia is her friendship with Clara. Laetitia's eyes are opened to Willoughby when Clara seeks her help on the grounds of their common womanhood in Chapter XVI. It is a "consciousness-raising" session in which the two women, superficially rivals, perceive the man as the common enemy. Here is the end of their dialogue:

> " Willoughby can imagine no other cause for my wish to be released. I have noticed it is his instinct to reckon on women as constant by their nature. They are the needles and he the magnet. Jealousy of you, Miss Dale! Laetitia, may I speak?"
> "Say everything you please."
> "I could wish--do you know my baptismal name?"
> "Clara."
> "At last! I could wish--that is, if it were your wish. Yes, I could wish that. Next to independence, my wish would be that. I risk offending you. Do not let your delicacy take arms against me. I wish him happy in the only way that he can be made happy. There is my jealousy."
> "Was it what you were going to say just now?"
> "No."
> "I thought not."
> "I was going to say--and I believe the rack would not make me truthful like you, Laetitia--well, has it ever struck you; remember, I do see his merits. I speak to his faithfullest friend, and I acknowledge he is attractive; he has manly tastes and habits. But has it never struck you--I have no right to ask. I know that men must have faults. I do not expect them to be saints. I am not one. I wish I were."
> "Has it never struck me?" Laetitia prompted her.
> "That very few women are able to be straightforwardly sincere in their speech, however much they desire to be?"
> "They are differently educated. Great misfortune brings it to them."
> "I am sure your answer is correct. Have you ever

known a woman who was entirely an Egoist?"

"Personally known one? We are not better than men."

"I do not pretend that we are. I have latterly become an Egoist, thinking of no one but myself, scheming to make use of every soul I meet. But then, women are in the position of inferiors. They are hardly out of the nursery when a lasso is round their necks, and if they have beauty, no wonder they turn it to a weapon and make as many captives as they can. I do not wonder! My sense of shame at my natural weakness and the arrogance of men would urge me to make hundreds captive, if that is being a coquette. I should not have compassion for those lofty birds, the hawks. To see them with their wings clipped would amuse me. Is there any other way of punishing them?"

"Consider what you lose in punishing them."

"I consider what they gain if we do not."

Laetitia supposed she was listening to discursive observations upon the inequality in the relations of the sexes. A suspicion of a drift to a closer meaning had been lulled, and the colour flooded her swiftly when Clara said: "Here is the difference I see--I see it. I am certain of it--women who are called coquettes make their conquests not of the best of men, but men who are Egoists have _good_ women for their victims, women on whose devoted constancy they feed; they drink it like blood. I am sure I am not taking the merely feminine view. They punish themselves too by passing over the one suitable to them, who could really give them what they crave to have, and they go where they--" Clara stopped. "I have not your power to express your ideas," she said.

"Miss Middleton, you have a dreadful power," said Laetitia.

I have quoted from this scene at length partly because it is a fine example of what Meredith's attentiveness to gesture can do so well--present us with the motions of the mind. Looking at Laetitia, Clara can formulate her terrible denunciation of Willoughby as a bloodsucker (especially terrible since Laetitia has just spoken of herself as "what the doctors call anaemic, a rather bloodless creature. The blood is life, so

I have not much life"). Listening to Clara, Laetitia learns something for real. Willoughby is no longer the same person for her. The women move from affection to renunciation of competition to a liberating formulation of their common oppression. Clara is relieved of her guilt at seeking her freedom, by seeing Willoughby's Egoism as much worse than her own. Laetitia is presented with another view of herself, not as suffering romantic heroine, but as victimized, exploited "good woman." It is significant that such a scene of friends coming to terms with a common problem, sharing affection and learning from one another, never occurs in Meredith's fiction between two men.

Although Laetitia's anaemia is appropriate as a comment upon Willoughby's use of women, and upon the unhealthiness of romantic delusions, it is still difficult to read about a childless, comfortable thirty year old woman so exhausted and wasted. It is a staggering sign of cultural sexism that Laetitia's sickliness is not completely absurd. The ending of the novel, however fitting it may be from the plot considerations described above, is also dissatisfying in its expectation that Laetitia's proclaimed exhaustion will induce us to ignore the dreariness of the life she has chosen. It is only the quite genuine economic situation, in which Willoughby is the only alternative to taking in pupils,[21]

---

[21] See pp. 185-6 and p. 614.

which makes the choice seem plausible to me. But again, it is at the expense of Laetitia's character. She is denied the energy to make a more creative change in herself and in her life in order to fit the demands of the plot, as well as the demands of her time.

A 1970's version of *The Egoist* would probably care more for Laetitia than for Clara. A rewriting might answer the questions of what happens underneath the romantic eyelids when the veil of illusion is torn away. Laetitia is economically and socially condemned to Willoughby. But the friendship between Clara and Laetitia today would result in something other than a double wedding ceremony. Two things would remain very much the same: Clara's exhilaration at her new powers, and the question formulated in the 80's and 90's as a response to Willoughby and Vernon and their counterparts in life: "Now that we have the New Women, where are the New Men?"

CHAPTER III

The Heroine of Reality: <u>Diana Of The Crossways</u>

-1-

When Yeats first met Maud Gonne in 1889 he described her to a friend as "a kind of Diana of the Crossways."[1] Presumably he meant to indicate that she was Irish, strikingly beautiful, articulate, passionately involved in politics, and living with confusing freedom. But though one can see how "Diana of the Crossways" was a good shorthand for such an anomaly as Maud Gonne must have been to contemporary eyes, it is truly dizzying to see a real radical organizer compared with a novel heroine who winds up married to an English minister for Irish affairs. It is also hard to bridge the generations between Diana's prototype, Caroline Norton, granddaughter of Sheridan, brought up in Windsor Castle and living always among the English aristocracy, making her way by virtue of her beauty and charm, and <u>despite</u> her passion and intelligence, and Yeats' beloved, formidable, industrious six-foot flesh and blood woman. <u>Diana of the Crossways</u> was published in 1885. Four years later it was certainly, for all the dizzying understatement of the connection, the best thing

---

[1] <u>The Letters of W.B. Yeats</u>, ed. Alan Wades (New York: 1955), p. 108; also quoted in Beer, p. 157.

around from which to start a description of a woman living with the force, energy, and freedom of Maude Gonne. It is not surprising that Yeats' mind leaped to a Meredithian heroine, and we should always keep in mind the six-foot figure of Maud Gonne as an indication of how very extraordinary the verbalness and intelligence and power of choice of Meredith's heroines appeared to a contemporary mind.

It is hard to imagine a nineteenth century novel capturing the breadth and scope of a life like Maud Gonne's. The ability to write about certain kinds of freedom always comes long after the practice. One need only call to mind the gap between George Eliot's life and the lives of her heroines. It takes one form of courage to conceive of living in a new way; it takes another form of courage, and time and experience as well, to shape new life configurations into the forms of fiction. Mary Ann Evans could not have walked into a George Eliot novel without throwing the whole structure into chaos.

<u>Diana of the Crossways</u> is itself an interesting example of the gap between experience and literary expression. Women were writing novels from the time of the birth of the genre in the last quarter of the seventeenth century. But nowhere does Mrs. Manly or Aphra Behn or Jane Austen or Charlotte Bronte or George Eliot choose for a heroine a woman self-supporting, living by her pen. Aphra Behn founded a major profession for the sex--in a world in which, as Jane Austen observed, marriage "was the only honourable provision for

well-educated young women of small fortune, and however uncertain of giving happiness, must be their pleasantest preservative from want."[2] The discovery of such a profession was therefore no small thing for women--yet the very women practicing it were silent on the meaning of their endeavor, often signing men's names to their work in order to obtain the serious attention which (as Mary Ellman has recently reminded us)[3] is still frequently refused to the writing of women. Certainly George Eliot and the Brontes felt they were putting on masculine garb when they took up their pens. Their silence on women as writers is a measure of how hard a fact it was for even those doing it to assimilate. It was an embarassment. It was something they blushed for. It was certainly not part of the universe as George Eliot described it, that Dorothea or Maggie could run off alone to London and join the editorial board of the Westminster Review. Such a chapter would destroy the boundaries of any woman's novel.

Meredith's choice of subject is a complicated question in itself, and before we have a closer look at how this unusual heroine comes off, we should stop and think about how he came to write this novel. In 1880 and 1885 Meredith published novels which, unlike all his other fiction, were retellings

---

[2] Pride and Prejudice, Volume I, Chapter 22.

[3] In Thinking about Women (New York: 1968).

of true events, even *romans à clef*. Since *The Tragic Comedians* and *Diana of the Crossways* are the only novels he ever wrote from life in quite this way I think we should ask what fascinated him in these stories so that he wanted to retell them as art? And since he wrote the two novels in succession I think it would be right to look for some similar matrix of material which compelled Meredith to work through the stories in his own terms.

The first novel, *The Tragic Comedians*, is really a novella and follows much more directly upon life than *Diana* does. It is in fact a "non-fiction novel." In 1879 Helene von Donniges published in German a book of reminiscences, *My Connection With Ferdinand Lassalle*.[4] In it she describes how her disputed engagement to the famous German socialist agitator of the '40's led to his death in a duel at the hands of Prince Yanko von Racowitza, later Helene's husband. A year after Helene's story appeared, Meredith published his fictionalized version of their romance.

To read Helene's account of the courtship and then turn to Meredith's novel is an exciting and unusual documentation of the creative process, for Meredith sticks very closely to Helene's scene by scene narration, even using verbatim snatches

---

[4] *Meine Beziehungen zu Ferdinand Lasalle* (1879). Not translated into English, but the same material is available in Part III ("Intoxication of Youth") of her autobiography, *Princess Helene von Racowitza: An Autobiography*, trans. Cecil Mar (New York: Macmillan, 1911).

of conversation, but he makes it all unmistakably his own. It is particularly astounding, for example, to hear him change Helene's Germanic, modern voice into a Victorian English rather Millamant-like tone. And Lassalle is, if anything, clearer and more present in Meredith's account than he is in that of his lover. But Meredith's primary manipulation of the story is to rescue a painfully arbitrary death, and give it the consequence and necessity of fiction.

Here is the core of the Lassalle-von Donniges story which Meredith retold using the names Sigismund Alvan and Clothilde von Runiger: Lassalle was a thirty-nine year old Jewish socialist activist, lover to a Countess Hatzfeld, a woman much older than he whom he had defended almost twenty years before against her brutish husband. Because of his politics, his religion, and his liaison with the countess he was an odd suitor for Helene, the twenty-year old daughter of a monarchist, attached to the court of the King of Bavaria. But he and Helene fell in love, persuaded that they shared a common mental life and were fated to the same destiny. After seeing very little of each other at long intervals, they met in the Alps by chance and spent a week together, at the end of which they became secretly engaged. When, on her return, Helene prematurely announced her engagement, her parents reacted violently and she fled in desperation to Lassalle expecting him to elope with her there and then. But Lassalle made the fatal mistake of ordering her to return to her parents' house. It was a dramatic gesture, made in front of her mother (who had discovered them at the house of a friend) in an attempt to win her parents' respect. Convinced that a man of his determination and eloquence could win round the parents once they knew him, Lassalle seems to have been too proud to start his married life without the usual bourgeois conventions. He wanted to play the role of the graciously received suitor in the family. But Helene, imprisoned by her brutal father, was weak enough to write renouncing Lassalle and even to denounce him to his own emissaries whom she mistakenly distrusted. Lassalle, formerly a bitter opponent of duelling, was so enraged by what he finally saw as Helene's treachery that he challenged her father to a duel. The father cleverly talked Helene's moony, slavish Rumanian sweetheart Yanko ("Marko" in the novel) into accepting the challenge for the family. Yanko, a boy of twenty who had never before held a pistol, went up against Lassalle, ready to sacrifice himself for Helene (or so he told her). Helene meanwhile finally saw her chance to escape from her father's house. She expected Yanko to be brought back dead or wounded, and she was ready to walk over his body (as she put it), or at least to take advantage of the commotion of his return to sneak away to her beloved Lassalle. Yanko however shot Lassalle in the genitals. In a post-Freudian age it is hard to accept Yanko's story that it was all an accident.

In any case, Lassalle died and Helene unpacked her bags and some months later married the unfortunate Yanko who died of consumption after five months of marriage. All in all, an unlikely choice of subject for an English novelist.[5]

The bare facts of Caroline Norton's story are considerably less melodramatic, although certainly painful. The beautiful Caroline Sheridan was the granddaughter of Richard Brinsley Sheridan and one of seven children. She had no dowry, since the Sheridans lost their shaky fortune in 1809, the year she was born, with the burning of the Drury Lane Theater, and her aimless father died when she was a child. At seventeen she married George Norton, a completely inappropriate choice. On her side it was purely a marriage of convenience. Norton, however, was infatuated with the witty and beautiful young girl. They both spent most of their lives suffering the consequences of their marriage. Norton was stupid, violent, jealous, and driven to extremes of all of these faults by the intelligence and especially the articulateness of his wife. In 1836, after ten years of marriage, they had a particularly violent quarrel, which ended by Norton locking his wife out of their house and sending their three

---

[5] Doris Lessing cites this novel as an anomaly among English fiction in the scope of action it presents. See "On the Golden Notebook" in *Partisan Review*, Winter, 1973, Vol. XI, No. 1.

young sons off to live with his sister in Scotland. Norton then tried to find some grounds for a divorce suit. He finally decided upon suing Lord Melbourne, the elderly Prime Minister and friend of his wife, for "criminal correspondance." It seems to have been an entirely cynical, mercenary gesture. Norton held a post through Melbourne's patronage, though Melbourne was a Whig and the Nortons fierce Tories. He had encouraged Caroline's friendship with the Prime Minister in the hope of continued favors. But Melbourne was particularly vulnerable to scandal of this sort for several reasons. He had been involved in a similar suit eight years before; he was known to have had many mistresses over the course of his life; he had been married to Lady Caroline Lamb, one of the most notorious of Byron's amours; and, most importantly, he was serving as head of state under a new virginal queen. We know from his later success at it how much Melbourne counted upon his ability to win the trust of the young Victoria. Norton who was always greedy, probably expected Melbourne to settle out of court for a large amount of money. The Tory party encouraged Norton in his suit in order to embarrass the head of the opposition. It was a scandal of national dimensions.

Through it all Caroline Norton had to keep silent. As a woman she had no legal existence in the case, except as she was incorporated in the legal person of her husband. She could not be represented by counsel at the trial. She could not defend herself against the charges of adultery. In the end the case was practically laughed out of court because of the obvious falsification of evidence on Norton's part. However, to have been named in such a scandal and to be living outside of her husband's house was enough to mar Caroline Norton's reputation for life. Only by the utmost powers of charm and through the use of her family connections in the aristrocracy was she able to maintain her social acceptability. And she never was accepted on the same terns as her respectable sisters. Men would not bring their wives to dine with her, and the upper middle classes (as against the lower aristocracy) considered her a pariah.

Worse than the social consequences, which Meredith details quite well for his Diana, were the personal consequences which Meredith omits. Caroline Norton was denied accessibility to her children for six years. Not until her youngest son died at the age of eight as the result of the neglect of his guardians did her husband relent and let the two surviving sons visit their mother regularly. Mrs. Norton was a passionate mother and it caused her terrible pain to have to fight with her husband for the occasional sight of her children. Norton knew this and kept the children from her in the hopes of forcing her to accept less support money from him. He also seized the money she earned from her poems, annuals, and novels, and he held her clothes, jewelry, and

books as his own property. In denying her access to her
children, and in using her property as his own, while
denying her support money, George Norton was entirely within
his rights. He was in fact a lawyer and used all the force
of the patriarchal English legal system against his wife.
She responded by working to change the law. Through her
vigorous and unprecedented publicizing of her personal wrongs
in private lobbying and in privately printed pamphlets,
Caroline almost singlehandedly got the Infant Custody Bill
passed in 1839, and later (after a second court fight with
Norton in 1853 in which he again tried to prove adultery with
Melbourne in order to rob her of an inheritance from her
mother) she greatly advanced the cause of the first Married
Women's Property Acts (1857).

Although she seems to have been unaware of it, Caroline
Norton was involved in another important political scandal.
In December 1845, Peel's government was secretly considering
total repeal of the Corn Laws. The story was leaked to the
press prematurely and it brought down the government. London
gossip attributed the leak to Mrs. Norton by way of her intimate friend, perhaps her lover, Sidney Herbert (Percy Dacier
in the novel). The story was not true, and from the fact
that she never denied it in print as she did quite stridently
every other slander ever aimed at her, it is possible that
Caroline never heard the rumors. But Herbert must have been

disturbed by the notoriety and must have realized that it might hinder his career, because shortly thereafter he broke with her and married his childhood sweetheart.

Meredith dealt with Mrs. Norton's story quite selectively. He gave her no children and he ended Diana's story with a blissful second marriage and pregnancy. (Mrs. Norton whom Meredith met once at the home of Lady Duff-Gordon, a common friend and the model for Emma Dunstane, did not remarry until a few months before her death in 1878). He left out the close ties of the Sheridan family and the vindictiveness of the Nortons. He had the miserable husband die young, though the real Mr. Norton lived on till all chance of another life for Caroline was finished. Most of all, he focused the novel around her friendship with Herbert and the Corn Laws scandal, which Meredith had probably heard denied by Lady Duff-Gordon.

This brings us to the points the two stories have in common: both are about famous and scandalous beauties, and both are about betrayals. Certainly the concentration in both stories upon the betrayal--Clothilde's renunciation of Alvan, Diana's sale of Percy's state secret--is an interesting pattern on the part of a betrayed husband. Meredith could have told either story from the point of view of the fiancé Yanko or the husband Norton ("Marko" and "Warwick" in the novels). He does not even interest himself in the sexual infidelity of his heroines. In both cases he makes the women far more virginal and guarded than they were. But he does make them betray their lovers (rather than their husbands) in other ways--through cowardice and recklessness if not through sexuality. And he centers his stories upon these acts of betrayal, and examines them closely from the woman's point of view.

Both women were considered too free and shocking in their manners, and yet they both wrote with sentimental conventionality about their lives. The fire and threat that people genuinely perceived in these two women, and that made them pariahs for most of their lives, is quite elusive to the modern reader of their own words. But in his novels Meredith reconstructs the heady sense of scandal and daring that surrounded Helene and Caroline. The cowardice of Clothilde, the recklessness of Diana, are clearly played out against the backdrop of the enormous social risk they are running in merely being who they are, talking as they talk, opening themselves to passion (rather than to sexual adventure). This is the nexus of what he was exploring in these novels, and it is clearly connected with his own memory of his wife's scandalous desertion with Henry Wallis.[6]

---

[6] In *Diana of the Crossways*, the infatuation of young Arthur Rhodes (who bears the name of Meredith's son by Mary) with the widowed Diana clearly reflects the young Meredith's courtship of the fascinating, aloof literary widow he eventually won.

Clothilde and Diana are not so much New Women, as women living in new circumstances. Clothilde proves no match for her circumstances because her conventionality and Lassalle's hold them back from breaking through social strictures to the Alpine freedom they crave. Diana on the other hand, learns to leave the dreams of the Alps, which represent her liberty, behind her, and accept a more conventional happiness. Both stories take as their core the <u>scandalousness</u> of their real life models, and focus on the essence of scandal--the opposition of the individual to the social values of her time and class. And as Meredith is above all a psychological novelist, the opposition is figured not merely as an outer struggle (Becky Sharpe against the World), but as a subtler struggle with the conventionality within and with the psychological pressures of living at the outer rim of society.

In the Lassalle story the key to it for Meredith, the facts which make the hero and heroine "tragic comedians," is this very split between their professed radicalism and romantic passion, and the cowardliness which leads them to put themselves under the control of a bigoted domestic tyrant. Helene and Lassalle--Clothilde and Alvan--won't take their happiness on its own terms. They insist upon reconciling it with the foolish values of the very social order--aristocratic and monarchical--which they want to overthrow. Oddly enough, their story is the exact reversal of the characteristic pattern I described in Chapter II of renunciation at the point of elopement. Perhaps because they were living Germans not English fictional characters, their renunciation brings the world down on their heads. Their real duty lay in running away. It is touching to think that in these two novels especially (although the pattern recurs in <u>Lord Ormont and his Aminta</u> and in <u>The Amazing Marriage</u>), Meredith is writing from Mary's point of view about the stakes involved in an elopement that cuts you off in some way from your social position and from your sense of yourself as a social being. Meredith never saw his wife after her elopement. He did not go to her deathbed. He hesitated to send their son to her. But he is perhaps in fiction seeking a kind of rapprochement, by seeking an understanding of what her life was after the rupture.

-2-

<u>Diana of the Crossways</u> is written in three parts. The first fourteen chapters deal with Diana's maidenhood, marriage, and the divorce action. The second part, the heart of the story (Chapters 15-36), deals with her romance with Percy Dacier, and ends with the Corn Laws scandal, Dacier's marriage, Warwick's death, and Diana's collapse. The third section (Chapters 37-43) brings her back to life and to her union with her true mate, the faithful Thomas Redworth. The links

that tie together this rather choppy story are Redworth, The Crossways (which is associated with her dead father, an Irish wit whom she loved), and Emma Dunstane. All three of these touchstones turn up at the crucial moments of decision in Diana's life. Emma is modelled after Lady Duff-Gordon, a friend of Meredith's who died in 1869, and whose daughter Janet Duff-Gordon Ross was a major infatuation of Meredith's life. Lady Duff-Gordon was from other accounts as selfless, intelligent, and resourceful as the Emma Dunstane of the novel, although the extraordinary friendship between Emma and Diana is Meredith's invention. The centrality of this friendship, however, does suggest that one of the things which interested Meredith about Mrs. Norton's story must have been the quality of the bond between the invalided Lady Duff-Gordon and the celebrated beauty.

The first third of the novel establishes Diana's precipitate marriage. Her husband, called Warwick, never appears directly and the marriage is made and broken off-stage. Instead of the courtship, we are given intimations of Diana's persecutions by several would-be lovers through the eyes of her older friend Emma. And worse still, we see what Emma does not, the indiscretion of Dunstane himself, a foolish, bluff, impulsive but goodhearted man, which frightens Diana away from the Dunstanes' estate, Copsley, a sort of second home to her, and into her hasty marriage. This motivation is entirely Meredith's invention, and so we should take it very seriously as an important part of what he saw as defining Diana's place in the world. That is, it is significant that he has his scandalous heroine begin by marrying for <u>protection</u> from the men around her.

The reasons for her estrangement from her husband are equally interesting. Meredith discreetly informs us that Diana attributes Warwick's actions largely to his bewilderment and humiliation at her refusal of sexual intimacy:

> They [Diana and Emma] spoke of the lawyers, and the calculated period of the trial; of the husband too, and his inciting belief in the falseness of his wife.
> "That is his excuse," Diana said, her closed mouth meditatively dimpling the corners over thoughts of his grounds for fury. He had them, though none for the incriminating charge. The sphinx mouth of the married woman at war and at bay must be left unriddled. She and the law differed in their interpretation of the dues of wedlock.[7]
>
> Those advocates of her opponent, in and out of court, compelled her honest heart to search within and own to faults. But were they not natural faults? It was her marriage; it was marriage in the abstract; her own mistake and the world's clumsy machinery of civilisation: these were the capital offender: not the wife who would laugh ringingly, and would have friends of the other sex, and shot her epigrams at the helpless despot, and was at times--yes, vixenish; a nature driven to it, but that was the word. She was too generous to recount her charges against the vanquished. If his wretched jealousy had ruined her, the secret high tribunal within her boson, which judged her guiltless for putting the sword

---

[7] p. 139. All citations are to the standard Memorial Edition of 1910, cited above, Volume 16.

> between their marriage tie when they stood as one,
> because a quarreling couple could not in honour
> play the embracing, pronounced him just pardonable.
> She distinguished that he could only suppose, man-
> likely, one bad cause for the division. (162)

To Warwick, Diana's sexual rejection can only be explained by her acceptance of a lover. Her complex emotional responses are not accessible to him and are simply not part of what he knows about her. Similarly, Sir Lukin Dunstane can forget her complete devotion to his wife when he tries to kiss her; we hear of a Lord Wroxeter as well who tries to battle a kiss from her. In focusing on the importance of these key experiences--with men in general, with the husband of her dearest friend, with her own husband, Meredith makes clear the purely external difficulties which burden Diana. To the men around her, despite the obvious strength of her personality which they all perceive and admire, her ideas, her emotions, her existence as an autonomous human being are never as real as her physical attractiveness. Meredith is particularly alert to the purely impersonal social consequences of Diana's beauty and her lack of male protection.

More importantly, he draws the inner toll of this social structure with great subtlety and skill. Sir Lukin's attack is a good case in point. Diana has gone for a walk in the woods with him, and she "remembered long afterward the sweet simpleness of her feelings as she took in the scent of wild flowers along the lands and entered the woods--

jaws of another monstrous and blackening experience" (44).
His gesture is soon blocked. Her indignation frightens
and abashes Sir Lukin immediately, and he goes from sentimental praise of her into equally mawkish self-accusation.
But it is a crushing, blackening experience for Diana:

> She was not the woman to take poor vengeance. But,
> oh! she was profoundly humiliated, shamed through
> and through. The question, Was I guilty of any
> lightness--anything to bring this on me? would not
> be laid. And how she pitied her friend! This
> house, her friend's home, was now a wreck to her;
> nay worse, a hostile citadel. The burden of the
> task of meeting Emma with an open face crushed her
> like very guilt. Yet she succeeded. After an hour
> in her bedchamber she managed to lock up her heart
> and summon the sprite of acting to her tongue and
> features; which ready attendant on the suffering
> female host performed his liveliest throughout the
> evening, to Emma's amusement and to the culprit
> ex-dragoon's astonishment; in whom, to tell the
> truth of him, her sparkle and fun kindled the sense
> of his being less criminal than he had supposed,
> with a dim vision of himself as the real proven
> donkey for not having been a harmless dash more so.(56)

With the same penetration and tact with which he dissected
Clara's feeling toward Willoughby, Meredith details Diana's
reaction to the attack: She feels humiliated and guilty,
"shamed through and through." In other words, she accuses
herself. We know that rape victims often feel this way (and
are treated as if guilty by male doctors and policemen).
Meredith understands that the toll of sexual objectification
is on the self-esteem of the objectified. Diana's sense of
defilement turns to guilt. But the circumstances don't
allow for her indulgence in guilt or sorrow (and certainly

not in healthy anger against her attacker). She must face
Emma. She must face Sir Lukin. She must put on a face and
act. Here is the beginning of the elaborate masquerade she
plays out in the second section of the novel for Percy Dacier.
Caroline Norton herself was loved by men and detested and
distrusted by certain women for precisely this quality: the
protective talent of masking emotional turmoil under the high
spirits of a socially aggressive, amusing woman.[8] It was not
insincerity, although certainly theatrical, for Caroline
Norton was also a woman who spoke to many people with disconcerting honesty about her domestic problems. But this
theatrical talent, which Meredith, who had a fair amount of
it himself, understands, is a means of survival in a situation
like Diana's in this scene or in later scenes with Dacier,
where she cannot betray emotions for which there is no social
place. For Caroline and Diana, the only way to survive in
society is to be an actress. I will come back to this
theatrical trick when we come to Diana's relation with Dacier,
but for now it is worth noting how Meredith picks up on the
emotional consequences for Diana of Sir Lukin's impulsiveness
(and indirectly of her social situation)--she is humiliated,
she feels a misplaced sense of guilt but little anger, and
she is forced to wear a mask.

---

[8] See Alice Acland <u>Caroline Norton</u> (London: 1948), pp. 208-9.

An interesting further development is the effect the mask has on Diana's relations with Emma. Sir Lukin interferes in the friendship, robbing Diana of the one person who could see through her outer composure and question her reasons for the marriage. It is noted later in the novel that Emma regrets Diana's coming to see her only in the company of other people. Emma dates this rupture from the time of the marriage, but the reader of course realizes that Sir Lukin not Warwick is the interloper. Diana's distance from Emma is throughout the novel the measure of her distance from herself, i.e. from self-knowledge and from her better self. She marries Warwick, then, in a fit of desperate alienation from her own nature.

Diana decides to marry Warwick partly because he is the present tenant of The Crossways and his money will preserve it for her. The decision is made at The Crossways, as is the more vividly presented decision to stay and face the charges of adultery Warwick later brings against her. Since the novel is built around these recurrent scenes at The Crossways it is worth pausing to examine this first of them in detail.

We are reminded of Vernon's meeting with Clara at the railway station (another kind of crossways). Here Redworth performs a similar function, calling a fleeing Diana back into Warwick's power, just as Vernon called Clara back into Willoughby's grasp. Diana wants to run away to America, be convicted of adultery, and so win a divorce from her hated husband. To contest the adultery charge is to contest the divorce. To preserve her name she must preserve her hated marriage. Emma sends Redworth to her with a melodramatic note telling Diana that she is risking her friend's life by running. Redworth rides through the darkness to find her. The double appeal is too much for Diana, and for reasons as unspecified as Clara's, she returns to bondage.

The situation has a double in the novel. Later on, Diana is on her way to the railway station, about to run away with Dacier, when Redworth summons her to Copsely to be with Emma for a dangerous, excruciating operation. Here Emma is genuinely in danger of death, and her danger saves Diana from the reckless gesture, for when Dacier and Diana meet in the moments after the operation the solemnity of the women's struggle against death, and the seriousness of their devotion to each other, breaks the mood of exhilaration and abandon necessary for flight.

The Crossways is invoked twice more: when Diana betrays Dacier's secret to the newspaper the chapter head describes a "Giddy Turn at the Spectral Crossways;" and when, recuperating from the sickness brought on by her husband's death and Dacier's desertion, she visits The Crossways with Emma to discover that Redworth has preserved all her auctioned belongings there for her in the hopes of her re-entering the house as his wife. The decisions involved in each of these Crossways scenes are very similar to Clara's decision at the railway station and partake of all the same ambiguities related to the conflicting demands of freedom and social order. The reiteration of the decision, however, puts this conflict very much at the forefront of the novel. Diana has to keep renegotiating the social contract for herself, and though she does have to learn renunciation and compromise each time, the solution to the dilemma is not nearly so important as the vivid, vital, rich presentation of the moment of choice. Insofar as this is a novel about scandal and betrayal, it is really about those moments and about the giddiness of trying to steer around those tricky turns.

The first directly presented Crossways scene is particularly significant in establishing the ambivalences and dangers of Diana's social position as a denounced wife. Redworth arrives at The Crossways uncertain of her innocence, and we see her through his eyes in a concrete and suggestive tableau:

> Danvers [the maid] had brought firewood and coal. Orders were given to her, and in spite of the opposition of the maid and the intervention of the gentleman, Diana knelt at the gate, observing, "Allow me to do this. I can lay and light a fire."
> He was obliged to look on: she was a woman who spoke her meaning. She knelt, handling paper, firewood, and matches, like a housemaid. Danvers proceeded on her mission, and Redworth eyed Diana in the first fire-glow. He could have imagined a Madonna on an old black Spanish canvas. (104)

The double aspect of servant and Spanish Madonna fixes Redworth's view of her character. It is interestingly Victorian that the housewifely image is invoked to establish her guiltlessness, and from there it is always an easy move to the Virgin. But the Spanish--i.e. the sensual--aspect of her figure is also important:

> The act of service was beautiful in gracefulness, and her simplicity in doing the work touched it spiritually. He thought, as she knelt there, that never had he seen how lovely and how charged with mystery her features were; . . . Elegant in plainness, the classic poet would have said of her hair and dress. She was of the women whose wits are quick in everything they do. That which was proper to her position, marked her appearance. Unaccountably this night, the fair fleshly presence over-weighed her intellectual distinction, to an observer bent on vindicating her innocence. Or, rather, he saw the hidden in the visible. (104-5)

Redworth responds to the sense of decorum about her which her clothing testifies to. The concreteness of the activity absolves Diana of Redworth's suspicion that she may be a sensualist. The absence of vanity in an "act of service" reveals her fundamental straightforwardness, her open, simple character. But at the same time he is seeing her beautiful features as "charged with mystery." The mystery is of course the doubt in his own mind raised by the scandal.

Diana's posture suggests prayer, and one is reminded of Mary Wollstonecraft's objection to similarly sexual descriptions of the charm of a woman praying.[9] Redworth's

---

[9] See **A Vindication of the Rights of Women** (1792) Chapter V.

(and Meredith's) interest is partially prurient--"voluptuous," Wollstonecraft would have called it. Diana is not presented here from within as a suffering, victimized woman--but externally as a romantic heroine made more beautiful by her danger. Redworth perceives not a woman lighting a fire, but a beauty in an appealing posture. Her actions are all seen through the lens of sexual desire. Indeed, Redworth's next impulse is to identify with Warwick:

> Owner of such a woman, and to lose her! Redworth pitied the husband.
> The crackling flames reddened her whole person. Gazing, he remembered Lady Dunstane saying of her once that in anger she had the nostrils of a war-horse. . . . She was now beset by battle. His pity for her, and his eager championship overwhelmed the spirit of compassion for the foolish wretched husband. . . . The question bit him: How far had she been indiscreet or wilful? And the bite of it was keen acid to his nerves. A woman doubted by her husband is always, and even to her champions in the first hours of the noxious rumour, until they have solidified in confidence through service, a creature of the wilds, marked for our ancient running. Nay more than a cynical world, these latter will be sensible of it. The doubt casts her forth, the general yelp drags her down; she runs like the prey of the forest under spotting branches; clear if we can think so, but it has to be thought in devotedness: her character is abroad. Redworth bore a strong resemblance to his fellowmen, except for his power of faith in this woman. Nevertheless it required the superbness of her beauty and the contrasting charm of her humble posture of kneeling by the fire to set him on the right track of mind. He knew and was sure of her. (105-106)

It is a wonderfully rich scene, for Diana appears with the ambiguity of life. She is a "creature of the wilds"--living beyond the boundaries, marked even in the eyes of her champion, alone with her in the cold bare house. She is homeless and, in the major metaphors associated with her, being tried by flame, hunted like an animal on the run. Her kneeling to the fire ends with it flaring up in the grate, bathing the Spanish Madonna in lurid light. It is a scene out of a Gothic novel. Yet at the same time as we are made aware of Diana's desperation, her mysterious looks, the sensual appeal of her posture, we are asked to see the homely simplicity of the gesture and the exposure of her position as touching evidence of her innocence. Redworth finds proof of her victimization partly in his own desires to victimize her, although this is not overtly stated; it is Diana's vulnerability which arouses Redworth and then pleads her innocence to him. The connection, a recognizable Gothic pattern, is one of Meredith's most penetrating and most poignant evocations of Diana's position. She is always, however innocent, a Madonna in the lurid flames, because of the effect of her beauty upon the men around her.

 Before we leave the first Crossways of Diana's life we should note that Redworth behaves much as Vernon did at the Railway station. He refuses to ask for Diana's promise that she will stay overnight, thereby throwing her upon her own sense of the dishonor of leaving. The social threat of running away is of course much clearer in Diana's case than it was in Clara's. It would be a major denial of her society to refuse to care for the verdict in an adultery trial.

Redworth's moment of sympathy with Warwick's rights of possession ("<u>owner</u> of such a woman") makes clear how impossible it is to flaunt them. Redworth the railway tycoon on his way into Parliament has more of a stake in the social order than that intellectual misfit Vernon. Redworth is above all the "practical" man, and to back him with Emma whose wisdom comes from her ill-health which gives her the perspective of eternity on her friend's affairs, is to make the scene more credible, but still unpleasant. Again a modern reader (and to a lesser extent a late Victorian reader as well) is much more willing than Meredith is to see Diana on the boat heading for America, where she has heard that women have more freedom. And again we wonder why a reminder of her free will in the matter should reinforce her sense of social obligation.

It is most relevant to remember in this connection that Meredith has altered the original story significantly here. Caroline Norton had no such choice. In the actual divorce case it was Melbourne ("Dannisburg" in the novel) who was served with a process. Mrs Norton could not defend herself in court because she had no legal existence apart from her husband; she could not defend herself in print because it would embarrass her friend and accused paramour and endanger his career. And she certainly could not leave the country since Norton was holding her children hostage against her.

t is important to remember the real case for two reasons.
'irst of all, it reminds us that Diana's claustrophobic
ocial position is in fact <u>understated</u>. Secondly, it focuses
ur attention upon Meredith's special interest in the story,
s a tale not of victimization or of illicit passion, but
f difficult moral choices; of a woman driven not to suf-
'ering or despair, but to continual self-questioning at the
:rossways.

-3-

In his description of Redworth watching Diana, Meredith
identifies Diana's scandalousness with her vulnerability.
We saw how her physical beauty affected the texture of her
life, causing her to run, to fight, to feel ashamed, and to
learn to act and mask her feelings. Now we have seen further
how male perception of this very vulnerability is erotic,
and forms an important part of the aura of mystery and
scandal that surrounds her. Diana's scandalousness, then,
is not a function of her own sexual desires; it is the
eroticism in the eyes of those beholding her.

Oddly enough, we see Diana bathed in flames, so to
speak, mostly through the eyes of her lovers, who know her
to be innocent. We've seen Redworth's momentary doubts. But
though Redworth wins her in the end, Diana's important lover
is Percy Dacier, a version of Sir Willoughby, a male egoist.

Dacier's perceptions of Diana vary wildly. He has three moments of clear insight into her character in tableaux which parallel the fire scene: the calm virginal trusting goddess Dian he sees at dawn by a hidden Alpine Lake; the pilloried angel who keeps midnight vigil beside the body of his uncle Lord Dannisburgh; the sweaty sturdy solemn human being emerging from Emma's operating room. Dacier holds these three tableaux in his head, but he is always liable to try to force them out when he has felt a blow to his pride (e.g. when she leaves him waiting at the railway station because she is rushing to Emma), and to substitute a cheap, reductive image of an actress and courtesan Diana. Because of Diana's past and her position as an estranged wife, Dacier is always having second thoughts about her which no proof of honesty and forceful character can erase. His icy capacity to deny his genuine experience of her and reduce her to a bluestocking or a flirt is frighteningly real.

Dacier breaks off with Diana over the ambiguities of her betrayal of his cabinet secret to the journalist Tonans. This is the trickiest part of the novel. Readers have always been puzzled by her motivation. There is an embarrassing flaw, which we must simply overlook if we are to read the novel sympathetically, in Meredith's willingness to have so politically involved and astute a woman misunderstand the consequences of premature publicity. It seems to me that

Meredith could surely not have made the same mistake with a male character. Although he must have heard the story of Mrs. Norton's betrayal of the imminent Corn Laws Repeal denied by Lady Duff-Gordon, Meredith seems to have thought the story true until after the novel appeared and provoked the resentment of Mrs. Norton's friends and relatives. Whether or not he believed the story, Meredith makes the betrayal of the secret the climax of the novel and the turning point of Diana's life. Since this is a difficult and subtle sequence, has caused so much trouble for readers and yet seems to be crucial of Meredith's conception of the novel-- the Crossways of Crossways, as it were--it seems well worth examining closely and in detail the scene which provides the motivation for her act.

Diana has been playing "Princess Egeria"[10] to Dacier, advising him on matters of state interest, enlivening him by her beautifully orchestrated dinner parties. Like Mrs. Ramsay, Diana is a great giver of dinners at which hostile and unsociable men learn to like each other. Meredith introduces the scene with Dacier by describing such a dinner. Diana's dinners are remarkable for eliminating the segregation of the sexes over brandy. Similarly, in one of her salon discussions

---

[10] "Princess Egeria" is Meredith's term for Diana and title of one of her novels. The reference is to Egeria, a nymph in Roman legend who instructed Numa in his wise legislation.

given in detail, the integration of male and female voices and the turn of the talk upon sexual differences is remarkable.[11] It is important to see her entertaining in this light--not a trivial amusement, but social pioneering and a performance of great brilliance. At the same time Diana's at home days and great dinners run her into terrible debt. She is running the enormous establishment for Dacier's benefit, with no hope of regularizing their union. In the chapter before, she is silently hopeful that her husband will die, but now that hope has been dashed by reports of his improving health.

The diners leave her to sit up late, staring at her empty bank book, and blocked over her writing, which is now a very pressing financial necessity. She has sold The Crossways (although it is Redworth who has secretly bought it). She cannot keep her head on the Meredithian comedy she is writing. Instead she feels restless and ready to write a romance full of "wicked princes, rogue noblemen, titled wantons, daisy and lily innocents, traitorous marriages, murders, a gallows dangling a corpse dotted by a moon, and a woman bowed beneath" (359-360). She is full of "a craving for excitement," of course the result of the enforced inactivity of her life, where she is forced to

---

[11] See Chapter XXVIII, pp. 261-5.

give and receive love only through abstract tokens.

At this moment Dacier arrives at her door asking for a midnight meeting. It is important to realize the real deceit of Dacier's return. He has come back with what he later thinks of as "pardonable cunning" to tease her with the news of the Corn Laws Repeal and to use the late hour and the great news as a way of breaking down the elaborate self-protective mask, her "queenly garb" (376) of sexual distance, which has marked the renewal of their friendship after the abortive elopement scheme. His approach is very clever:

> Diana stood at the door. "Have you forgotten anything I ought to know?"
> He came up to her and shut the door softly behind her, holding her hand. "You are near it. I returned. . . . But tell me first: You were slightly under a shadow this evening--dejected."
> "Did I show it?"
> She was growing a little suspicious, but this cunning touch of lover-like interest dispersed the shade.
> "To me you did."
> "It was unpardonable to let it be seen."
> "No one else could have observed it."
> Her woman's heart was thrilled; for she had concealed the dejection from Emma.
> "It was nothing," she said; "a knot in the book I am writing. We poor authors are worried now and then. But you?" (361-2)

Meredith is careful to show us Dacier's "<u>cunning</u> touch of lover-<u>like</u> interest " (italics mine), working to undermine Diana's suspicions at this midnight return. Dacier's statement (probably a pretense) that he has seen some distress on Diana's face during the dinner party we have just watched

her brilliantly command, is of course ironic in the light of
her very real distress over her writing--that is, over the
livelihood she needs to keep giving him brilliant dinner
parties. But Dacier has no real penetration of her character
and circumstances. In fact, when, after the fiasco of the
disclosure, she finally does tell him of her financial difficulties, incurred for his sake, he can hardly understand
what she means, and he cannot at all understand why her
pride should make it impossible for her to appeal to him for
money. So the scene begins with a quietly ironic reiteration of the terrible double bind she is in.

Having lulled her fears, Dacier begins to tease her:

> His face rippled by degrees brightly, to excite
> a reflection in hers.
> "Shall I tune you with good news? I think it
> will excuse my coming back."
> "Very good news?"
> "Brave news, as far as it goes."
> "Then it concerns you!"
> "Me, you, the country."
> "Oh! do I guess?" cried Diana. "But speak,
> pray; I burn."
> "What am I to have for telling it?"
> "Put no price. You know my heart. I guess,
> or fancy. It relates to your chief?"
> Dacier smiled in a way to show the lock without
> the key; and she was insensibly drawn nearer to him,
> speculating on the smile.
> "Try again," said he, keenly appreciating the
> blindness of his motive of her studious dark eyes,
> and her open-lipped breathing. (362)

Meredith focuses on the visual contrast of Dacier's lips,
calculatingly closed, and Diana's lips, naively opening.
Again Dacier's voluptuous observation of her excitement is

very like the voyeurism of Gothic novels. Diana is involved out of humanitarian compassion (the long overdue Repeal of the Corn Laws lowered bread prices and its direct cause was the terrible Irish Potato Famine), and out of interest in his grand career, which she imagines to be guided by the same ideals. He is coyly bargaining for kisses with great news of relieved mass suffering, not mere juicy political gossip. Notice how his mouth ripples not with any real joy at the news, which he appears indifferent to, but as a ploy to seduce her interest.

After some more teasing, Dacier finally tells Diana that his minister is to call Parliament together for the next month and ask for total repeal.

> Diana clapped hands; and her aspect of enthusiasm was intoxicating. "He is a wise man and a gallant minister! And while you were reading me through I was blind to you," she added meltingly.
> "I have not made too much of it?" said he.
> "Indeed you have not."
> She was radiant with her dark lightnings, yet wholly subject to him under the spell of the news he had artfully lengthened out to excite and overbalance her; and her enthusiasm was all pointed to his share in the altered situation, as he well knew and was flattered in knowing. (362-3)

His cunning is paying off now--she remains touched by his lover-like interest in her emotions; his artful lengthening out of the news has excited her, melted, overbalanced; and now he is ready to try the next step, which he introduces by the use of her pet name, "Tony" which she has forbidden him to use since it is associated with their abortive elopement. At first she doesn't notice because of her exhilaration. She has been looking for melodramatic excitement, and here it is.

> "So Tony is no longer dejected? I thought I could freshen you and get my excuse."
> "Oh! a high wind will make a dead fly like a bird. I soar. Now I do feel proud. I have longed for it--to have you leading the country: not tugged at like a waggon with a treble team uphill. We two are a month in advance of all England. You stand by him?--only to hear it, for I am sure of it!"
> "We stand or fall together."
> Her glowing look doated on the faithful lieutenant.
> "And, if the henchman is my hero, I am but a waiting woman. But I must admire his leader."

She is indulging in the sort of sentimentality Meredith was always alert to, worshipping the cold politician as if he were a gallant knight. At the same time she does feel proud at being part of a moment of history she has longed for, and at feeling a sort of culmination of her relation with Dacier. For the tacit terms of their new connection dictate no talk of love, but political counsel on her part and confidences on his instead; so this enormous secret is a very special moment, a spectacular love token for her. But Diana's censored passion is slipping out as mere silly gush, which makes Dacier think he has her right where he wants her. The scene continues with his big move:

> "Tony!"
> "Ah! no"--she joined her hands, wondering where armed majesty had fled--"no softness! no payments! Flatter me by letting me think you came to a head-- not a silly woman's heart, with one name on it, as it has not to betray. I have been frank; you need

> no proofs. . ." The supplicating hands left her
> figure an easy prey to the storm, and were crushed
> in a knot on her bosom. She could only shrink.
> "Ah! Percy. . . .you undo my praise of you--my
> pride in receiving you."

Only now does she remember his first intimation that he wanted "payment" for the secret. The cry to be thought of as "a head" is particularly pathetic, although it is in the twentieth century such a cliché of romantic dialogue it is hard to respond freshly to it. But it has been her vanity to believe that she has been helping the great man forward by her intellect, and she has been indulging very strongly in that fantasy of herself as "waiting woman" to her "hero." But her being "visibly subject" to him means something else to the hero himself. Diana is genuinely confused because she and Percy have two chapters back indirectly talked of her husband's death and so her immediate response is "I have been frank." She is puzzled by his need for physical proofs. But, of course, her majesty of bearing, her tact and control so painfully achieved amid emotional and economic turmoil, have been more real to him than her intellectual companionship.

Percy is not looking for great physical passion, however, as is evident by the next two pages of conversation which elapse between this embrace and the climactic kiss which so traumatizes Diana. For a while they just stand there:

>They were speechless perforce.
>
>"You see, Tony, my dearest, I am flesh and blood after all."
>
>"You drive me to be ice and door-bolts!" Her eyes broke over him reproachfully.
>
>"It is not so much to grant," he murmured.
>
>"It changes everything between us."
>
>"Not me. It binds me the faster."
>
>"It makes me a loathsome hypocrite."
>
>"But, Tony! is it so much?"
>
>"Not if you value it low."
>
>"But how long do you keep me in this rag-puppet's state of suspension?"
>
>"Patience!"
>
>"Dangling and swinging day and night!"
>
>"The rag-puppet shall be animated and repaid if I have life. I wish to respect my hero. Have a little mercy. Our day will come; perhaps as wonderfully as this wonderful news. My friend, drop your hands. Have you forgotten who I am? I want to think, Percy."
>
>"But you are mine."
>
>"You are abasing your own."
>
>"No, by Heaven!"
>
>"Worse, dear friend; you are lowering yourself to the woman who loves you."
>
>"You must imagine me superhuman."
>
>"I worship you--or did."
>
>"Be reasonable Tony. What harm! Surely a trifle of recompense? Just to let me feel I live! You own you love me. Then I am your lover."
>
>"My dear friend Percy, when I have consent to be your paramour this kind of treatment of me will not want apologies." (363-4)

Dacier's speech is full of romantic clichés, Diana's straight to the point and honest. It is very similar to the dialogues between Sir Willoughby and Clara ("Could you be mine after death?" "Married is married I think."). Diana's abruptness punctures Percy's stylized pretensions. She mimics his metaphor of the puppet--absurd for such a magisterial man; and finally she puts his romantic blathering into plain English (or at least as plain as we can expect in a Victorian novel) with the charged word "paramour." It is worth noticing, too, that Dacier's basic claim is one of ownership: "But you are mine." It is certainly not passion that motivates him, as his claim for "flesh and blood" (another cliché which she parodies) only makes all the more apparent. Here is Dacier's reaction to Diana's final shot:

> The plain speaking from the wound he dealt her was effective with a gentleman who would never have enjoyed his privilege had he been of a nature unsusceptible to her distinct wish and meaning.

Which, translated, means her hurt protest that she is not his mistress cuts him, because like Sir Willoughby, he values sexual coldness in women. "Privileges" is deliberately ambiguous here. Meredith means both the privilege of being admitted regularly to Diana's house, and also the privileges (or "liberties") he is taking with her person.

But now he begins to whimper. Diana is at the same time regaining her vitality, and her "queenly garb."

> He sighed. "You know how my family bothers me. The woman I want, the only woman I could marry, I can't have."
> "You have her in soul."
> "Body and soul it must be! I believe you were made without fire."
> "Perhaps. The element is omitted with some of us--happily some think. Now we can converse. There seems to be a measurement of distance required before men and women have a chance with their brains--or before a man will understand that he can be advised and seconded. When will the cabinet be consulted?"
> "Oh a few days. Promise me. . ."
> "Any honourable promise!"
> "You will not keep me waiting longer than the end of the Session?"
> "Perhaps there will be an appeal to the country."

> "In any case, promise me: have some compassion."
> "Ah, the compassion! You do not choose your words, Percy, or forget who is the speaker."
> "It is Tony who forgets the time she has kept her lover dangling. Promise, and I will wait."
> "You hurt my hand, sir."
> "I could crack the knuckles. Promise!"
> "Come to me tomorrow."
> "Tomorrow you are in your armour--triple brass! All creation cries out for now. We are mounted on barbs, and you talk of ambling."
> "Arthur Rhodes might have spoken that."
> "Rhodes!" he shook off the name in disgust. "Pet him as much as you like; don't. . ." he was unable to phrase his objections.
> She cooled him further with eulogies of the chevaleresque manner of speaking which Mr. Rhodes could assume; till for very wrath of blood--not jealousy: he had none of any man with her; and not passion; the little he had was a fitful gust--he punished her coldness by taking what hastily could be gathered. (364-6)

Dacier's fit of passion is anger at not being given what is his. It is Diana's self-command that infuriates him; notice that he loses the power of speech as she gains her tongue. He had planned a seduction but when called at that game (by the word "paramour"), he violates her--for the gesture is indeed a violation. Readers who see Diana as sexually cold are mistaken. As Meredith says after the kiss, "she was never prudish, only self-respecting." She pretends to be without fire in order to maintain the distance from him which will allow them to see each other. But it is Dacier who is passionless and therefore unable to sustain his attachment for her without a direct sign of possession. He is flattered and fascinated by Diana, but he is not in love with her. An egoist, he is in love with the notion of himself as her lover. That is why Arthur Rhodes is a particularly infuriating subject; for the puppyish Rhodes is a perfect parody of the silliness and narcissism of Dacier's idea of love-talk. Diana starts coming back to herself by coming to an awareness of the quality of his speech. By comparing him to Rhodes she is indeed striking home. He kisses her <u>to put her in her place</u>.

And it works:

> Her shape was a pained submission; and she thought: where is the woman who ever knows a man! as women do think when one of their artifices of evasion with a lover, or the trick of imposingness, has apparently been subduing him. . . as she did with Sir Lukin, Diana takes the blame upon herself:
> ". . . the fault is mine when I am degraded. I trust you; there's the error. . . ."
> "Trust me you may," he said. "But you know we are one. The world has given you to me, me to you. Why should we be asunder? There's no reason in it."
> She replied: "But still I wish to burn a little incense in honour of myself, or else I cannot live. It is the truth. You make death my truer friend, and at this moment I would willingly go out. You would respect me more dead than alive. I could better pardon you too."

Diana, who is elsewhere identified with Clarissa,[12] is indeed fighting Clarissa's battle here. And Dacier is Lovelace here as he pleads "for the red mouth's pardon" while secretly thinking he has deserved the "crumbs" he has gathered

---

[12] Diana sails on the yacht Clarissa in Chapter XV in order to escape her husband's attempt to obtain his legal rights of cohabitation after his adultery suit is unsuccessful.

there by force. The scene makes explicit the stakes of Clarissa's battle: not sexual purity but self-respect (for her) and power (for him). Diana says here that she must burn a little incense to herself or die. At other times she says she needs to be able to kiss Emma frankly, and so is glad to have been saved from the elopement with Dacier, despite her passion for him. Both statements emblemize the devastation she feels when she loses her respect for herself. This is the important stake Dacier is gambling with so lightly. To one without social sanctions, without a place to call home, self-respect is the last stronghold of the ego. Dacier has violated her sense of herself as an honorable woman.

After Dacier leaves, full of comfortable reflections on his victory, Diana returns to face her empty bank book and her bogged down manuscript once more, and discovers that she is desperate with her loss of self-esteem:

> Would Percy have humiliated her so if he had respected her? He took advantage of the sudden loss of her habitual queenly initiative at the wonderful news to debase and stain their intimacy. The lover's behavior was judged by her sensations: she felt humiliated, plucked violently from the throne where she had long been sitting securely, very proudly. . . . She was a dethroned woman. Deeper within an unmasked actress, she said. Oh she forgave him! But clearly he took her for the same as other women consenting to receive a privileged visitor. And, sounding herself to the soul, was she so magnificently better? Her face flamed. She hugged her arms at her breast to quiet the beating, and dropped them when she surprised herself embracing the memory. He had brought political news,

>and treated her as--name the thing! Not designedly,
>it might be; her position invited it. "The world
>had given her to him." The world is always a pro-
>phet of the mire; but the world is no longer an
>utterly mistaken world. She shook before it.
>
>She asked herself why Percy or the world should
>think highly of an adventuress, who was a denounced
>wife, a wretched author, and on the verge of bank-
>ruptcy. (369-370)

Her sense of humiliation is intimately connected with her need for money. This is what sends her off to the newspaper office, thinking of "her fortunes recovered, disgrace averted, hours of peace for composition stretching before her; a summer afternoon's vista" to replace the midwinter midnight she is living in. The quite foggy motivation is admittedly confusing on the surface. But I think it is very striking in its psychological validity. It is not a rational gesture on Diana's part to run out the door and sell the news to Tonans to make up for Dacier's kiss, but it is certainly appropriate.

Dacier's crass treatment of her leaves Diana totally disoriented. It reveals the shaky foundations of her life in London--trusting in Dacier without thinking too clearly of their situation, trusting in the future, which means hoping for either her husband's death or her own seduction. She has been living entirely for Dacier, thinking for his sake, writing for his sake, even selling her beloved Crossways. But he thinks of her not as a noble comrade, but as a mistress. Dacier's act of violation puts her in a psychological trap. She cannot be angry with him (remember that she couldn't even be angry with Sir Lukin!) for he is the center of her life and she cannot afford to estrange herself from him. She has built her life around her respect for him; "I worship you--or did" she tells him. His insulting behavior takes away her last props.

Getting money from an important editor is Diana's way of regaining self-esteem partly because her bankruptcy is emblematic of her emotional investment. Worse, she realizes she is only one step away from literally asking him for money. Her bankruptcy makes her an adventuress. But if she can make money on her own, earn thousands of pounds taking control of her own situation in life, then she is not dependent on her lover. Meredith explains her blindness to the real significance of the action by pointing to the perilous position she sees herself in.

> When we are losing balance on a precipice we do not
> think much of the thing we have clutched for support. . .
> We stand as others do, and we will for the future be
> warned to avoid the dizzy stations which cry for
> resources beyond a common equilibrium, and where a
> slip precipitates us to ruin. (382)

Dacier leaves her house calmly thinking of affairs of state, feeling for the future content to "play second to her sprightly wits in converse" now that "he had some warm testimony to his mastery over her blood." He can now be more at ease with "enthusiastic friends" who "had congratulated him," having satisfied the "thirst of the lover, whose pride, irritated by confidential wild eulogies of the beautiful woman, had recently clamoured for proofs of his commandership" (345). In the simplest terms, then, Percy has asserted his power over Diana, humiliating her so deeply that she has to immediately right the balance by earning some money. It is a very modern situation. And it is not hard to imagine that Clarissa's life would have been different if she had anything other than her body to sell in order to live in the world.

 The ride to the newspaper office is significant of the emotional content of Diana's gesture. She and her maid Danvers risk the very frightening, unconventional act of appearing alone on a London street at night. The attitude of the cabman is respectful but it is a dangerous situation, and Danvers is astounded that her mistress can look out the the window and comment on a brawl between street-walkers and clinets. That is the population beyond their London house but it is certainly not to be seen, and much less to be spoken of by a lady. In the newspaper office Danvers is further dismayed when the rushing, newspapermen ignore her, and do not bow and nod as gentlemen do to ladies in society. It is extremely disorienting to be "a disregarded object" without the customary "homage to the sex" (301).

 Readers have complained about Meredith's refusal to dramatize the scene between Tonans and Diana. But it is much more to the point to show us Danvers disregarded in the lobby than to try to make Diana's absurd political blunder more vivid. For Diana has been struggling with Danvers' situation since her marriage began to fall apart. She had to earn money and live without the ease and condescension due to a lady. As a result, she is no longer dependent upon the protection of men. Her actual separation brought her in contact with the London streets, where the price of independence is just more explicit. "Cupid's footpads" as she calls the men who disturb her on her walk, become a regular part of her life. Emma asks her how she can choose an unprotected life in London lodgings:

> "Let me be independent! Besides, I begin to learn something of the bigger world outside the one I know, and I crush my mincing tastes. In return for that I get a sense of strength I had not when I was a drawingroom exotic. Much is repulsive. But I am taken with a passion for reality." (139)

Diana's mistaken trip to the newspaper office partakes of the same gallantry. She is willing to mix with a new reality beyond her sheltered sphere, and she is strengthened by the brush with rough truths, especially since that seems to be the price of her freedom.

Jane Eyre runs similar risks for the same stakes. Like Diana she cannot live unless she can burn a little incense in honor of herself. When Rochester points out that there is no one to care one way or the other if she is his legal wife, she cries out at him "I care for myself!" and runs out of the door to face exposure and near starvation rather than live entirely dependent upon the good will of her lover.

Jane Eyre realizes that it would be hard for her to maintain her sense of herself as Rochester's wife; but as his mistress it would be impossible. Diana is running away from the same servitude when she rushes out into the London streets at midnight to sell her secret.

Nothing I can say can obviate the problem of her political naiveté. But it should be no longer a mystery that Meredith focused upon this probably baseless anecdote about Mrs. Norton as the center of his novel. I said before that in <u>The Tragic Comedians</u> and in <u>Diana of the Crossways</u> he centered on the acts of betrayal, as if reexamining something of Mary Nicolls Meredith's state of mind when she left him for Wallis. In <u>The Tragic Comedians</u>, Clothilde betrays Ferdinand out of cowardice. Meredith points with big arrows to the root of her betrayal: her surrender of her will to her Ferdinand, which prepares the way for surrender to her father. Meredith did not need to make the Freudian connections we would now, for he came at it instead through his infallible instinct for the power relations between lovers.

Diana is reckless rather than cowardly. She is too ready to run off to the continent at her first Crossways, to run away with Dacier later on, to run off into the night to make some money, and finally to run away from her real love for Redworth. But Meredith locates this recklessness in a fear of subordination, a refusal to submit to humiliating circumstance, a love of honesty and independence that is the opposite of Clothilde's willess subservience. She strikes out each time, however mistakenly, in the service of her own freedom. She is always pushing against the social pressures which sent Clara driving back to Patterne Hall from the railway station, although like Clara she is always driving back again from her Crossways into the society. Both Diana and Clothilde are betrayed by their lovers and respond by betraying them in turn. But unlike the bourgeois Clothilde, Diana is fighting for self-respect out in the streets, where she has only to look about her to see the fate of the woman who leaves herself with nothing but her body to sell. Diana is selling Dacier's secret in order to avoid being a prostitute--she is betraying him in order to keep her freedom. At the moment of her betrayal she hardly thinks of her responsibility to him. She is too busy fighting for her own life. What makes <u>Diana of the Crossways</u> a feminist novel, despite its soppy ending and despite the impossibility of seeing Diana as a wholly liberated woman (her contemporary Ibsen's Nora is a good touchstone here) is Meredith's fully realized sense of the stakes that Diana is playing for, of the dangers of loss of self-esteem, of deep humiliation, and of social ostracism, which she is running; in other words, his acknowledgement of the recklessness she would of course feel as a woman living at the very boundaries of the permissible.

The scene in which Diana decides to ride out to the newspaper office takes place in her dressingroom. It is very much like the scene in Emma, (Part I, Chapter 16) after Mr. Elton's unexpected declaration of love, which teaches Emma a similar lesson about the disjunction between social realities and private fantasies. Meredith may well have had Austen in mind here. In any case the scenes are quite similar, with the one big difference that Emma is left alone by her maid to look in her mirror; but Danvers leaves Diana to face her writing. It is the sententiousness of the last sentence she has penned which she finds self-accusatory, rather than any remembered improper word or gesture. Her stilted prose represents the double face she has been presenting even to herself. The novel, called <u>The Man of Two Minds</u>, seems to be modelled on her misperception of Redworth[13] but in fact ironically parallels her affair with Dacier insofar as it presents a man wishing to remake his fiancee after his own ideal of womanhood. The novels which Diana writes are sketched out enough so that we see

---

[13] Diana assumes that Redworth is in love with her protegee, Miss Paynham, a sad dull woman who has been deserted by her lover and is received only by Diana whose own misfortunes have made her compassionate toward such a social outcast. The situation is parallel to that between Mr. Elton, Harriet, and Emma, except that in <u>Diana</u> the heroine sits for rather than paints the portrait which provides the occasion for the confusion. As in the case of Emma, Diana's delusion about Redworth is a sign of her lack of self-knowledge.

their appropriateness to her mind and to her stage of life--
her situation, her pressures, her misperceptions of herself
and her friends. It is a long way to go to place your heroine in her dressing room with her novel in front of her instead of her mirror. Although Diana ends the novel pregnant
and not writing, throughout the novel her own books have
made clear the seriousness of her intellectual life--she is
not merely engaged in an education in decorum preparatory to
marriage, as are so many English heroes and heroines. She
is actively reordering her reality into a continuing serious
effort to take her life in her own hands. If Emma had been
writing novels in that dressing room, Mr. Knightley need
not have been so perfect.

The parallel with Emma is intriguing again when we remember that "Emma" is the name of Diana's dearest friend, who
is in a relation to her very like that of Mrs. Weston to Emma
Woodhouse. This friendship is the other important way in
which Meredith makes us believe in the seriousness of Diana's
decisions. The men in the novel are really mere ciphers.
Dacier's character is interestingly drawn--he is in many
ways the most intriguing version of the Austin/Willoughby
character--and Redworth is certainly less of a disaster than
Vernon Whitford, if only because he is given some almost
real sexuality. But Dacier and Redworth exist like Dora and
Agnes in <u>David Copperfield</u>, as poles on some landscape of

moral growth and maturity that Diana walks through. The more she idolizes Dacier, the more she hates herself, and the closer she is to dishonour and death. The more she likes Redworth, the more realistic, wholesome, and vital and the less sentimental she is. Their major role is to keep these attitudes toward life clearly defined for Diana to choose between.

But Emma's role is very special. The friendship between the two women is detailed and bears the weight of very heavy plot lines: I have mentioned above how Diana's chastity is saved and her self-knowledge measured by her relationship with Emma. In A Room of One's Own, written more than fifty years after Diana was published, Virginia Woolf wrote of the great feat it would be to write a novel about two women who work together in a lab and like each other.[14] Meredith is quite close to writing such a novel in 1885 when he works to describe a genuine friendship between two brilliant women. He occasionally sentimentalizes their speech, especially putting stilted language into Emma's mouth. Sometimes he has them speak in self-conscious abstractions and they are too concerned with "Friendship" as a religion. This sort of exaggerated utterance seems to me to be more characteristic

---

[14] A Room of One's Own, Chapter 5. In the context of this discussion of friendship between women in literature Virginia Woolf tries "to remember any case in the course of my reading where two women are represented as friends." The only work she names is Diana.

of male friendships than of friendship between women. But it is nevertheless a very moving portrayal of a very difficult thing to catch. Emma's loving attempts to construe her Tony's state of mind from evasive letters are very well done. Diana's sense of her friend as a moral force to be always reckoned with is also very fine. And best of all is the final sequence in which Emma nurses Diana back to life, and judges the pace of the recovery by the action of her friend's mind. She doesn't believe that all is well until she sees Diana's wits engaged with characteristic force and clarity.

Perhaps most surprising is the way the novel ends, in a tableau once more, this time of the two women clasping hands watching the sunset, thinking of Emma's death and Diana's child. It is a wonderfully imaginative stroke, and exactly right in its way. For the real intimacy in the novel is the intimacy between the two women. Redworth and Diana will be happy together, but they are never going to be as fully understanding of each other and as united in sympathies as the two women are. The ending is surprising, but appropriate. It seems to me another striking example of Meredith's deeply felt feminism that he conceived of the intellectual and emotional relationship between the two women as primary.

In the introductory chapter of the novel Meredith glances at what seems to be the Preface to _Pendennis_ which I referred to in Chapter I, in which Thackeray laments his inability to present fully animated puppets because his readers could not take the full truth.[15] It was very much on Meredith's mind in this particular novel that he was creating a different sort of heroine--a heroine with brains, he exclaims in a letter.[16] In the novel he speaks of her as the Heroine of Reality. Constance Asper, Dacier's cold, prayerful, pampered wife, says Meredith, is the true Heroine of Romance, by which he means both the traditional novel heroine and the masculine cultural ideal of femininity. The essential difference between the Heroine of Reality and the Heroine of Romance is the freedom to make moral choices, to experience the giddiness of the Crossways. In writing <u>Diana of the Crossways</u>, Meredith is asking us to accept in fiction a different sort of heroine, and in life, a different model of the female heroic:

> Poor Diana was the flecked heroine of Reality: not always the same; not impeccable; not an ignorant innocent, nor a guileless; good under good leading; devoted to the death in a grave crisis; often wrestling with her terrestrial nature nobly; and a growing soul; but not one whose purity was carved in marble for the assurance to an Englishman that his possession of the changeless thing defies time and his fellows--is the pillar of his home and universally enviable. Your fair one of Romance cannot suffer a mishap without a plotting villain, per-

---

[15] See p.   above.

[16] <u>Letters</u>, Vol. III, 731.

chance many of them, to wreak the dread iniquity;
she cannot move without him; she is the marble
block, and, if she is to have a feature, he is the
sculptor; she depends on him for life, and her
human history at least is married to him far more
than to the rescuing lover. No wonder, then, that
men should find her thrice cherishable featureless,
or with the most moderate possible indication of a
countenance. Thousands of the excellent simple
creatures do; and every reader of her tale. On the
contrary, the heroine of Reality is that woman you
have met or heard of once in your course of years,
and very probably despised for bearing in her composition the motive principle; at best, you say, a
singular mixture of good and bad; anything but the
feminine ideal of man. She is shamelessly independent of the world's wickedness. Feature to some
excess, you think, distinguishes her. Yet she fur-
nishes not any of the sweet sensual excitement per-
taining to her spotless rival pursued by villainy.
She knocks at the doors of the mind, and the mind
must open to be interested in her. Mind and heart
must be wide open to excuse her sheer descent from
the pure ideal of man. (399-400)

BIBLIOGRAPHY

Works By George Meredith

Meredith, George. Letters of George Meredith. Edited by C. L. Cline. 3 Vols. Oxford: Clarendon, 1970.

Meredith, George. Works. "Memorial Edition," 29 Vols. New York: Scribner's, 1909-1912. (But this edition has the weaker version of Richard Feverel.)

Meredith, George. The Ordeal of Richard Feverel. New York: Modern Library, Random House, 1950. (This edition is based on the 1859 text.)

Other Works

Acland, Alice. Caroline Norton. London: Constable, 1948.

Barrie, Sir James Matthew. George Meredith: A Tribute. Portland, Me: Thomas Mosher, 1919. 950 copies printed.

Bartlett, Phyllis. "Richard Feverel, Knight-Errant." BNYPL, 63 (1959), 329-40.

Beach, Joseph Warren. The Comic Spirit in George Meredith. New York: Longmans, 1911; rpt. 1963.

Beer, Gillian. Meredith: A Change of Masks. London: Athlone Press, 1970.

Buchen, Irving H. "The Importance of Minor Characters in The Ordeal of Richard Feverel." BUSE, 5 (1961), 154-66.

Clark, Alice. Working Life of Women in the Seventeenth Century. New York: Dutton, 1919.

Currin, Frank. "Adrian Harely--the Limits of Meredith's Comedy." NCF, 8 (1953), 272-282.

Daiches, David. "Samuel Richardson." Literary Essays. Edinburg and London: Oliver and Boyd Ltd., 1966, pp. 26-42; reprinted in Twentieth Century Interpretations of "Pamela." New Jersey: Prentice-Hall, 1969, pp. 14-25

Ekeberg, Gladys W. "The Ordeal of Richard Feverel as Tragedy." CE, 7 (1946), 387-393.

Ellmann, Mary. Thinking about Women. New York: Harcourt Brace Jovanovich, 1968.

Evans, Elizabeth E. Ferdinand Lassalle and Helene von Donniges: A Modern Tragedy. London: Swan Sonnenschein & Co., 1897.

Fletcher, Ian., ed. Meredith Now: Some Critical Essays. New York: Barnes & Noble, 1971.

Forman, Maurice Buxton., ed. George Meredith: Some Early Appreciations. 1909; rpt. London: Methuan, 1970.

Galland, Rene. George Meredith and British Criticism: 1851-1909. Paris: Les Presses Francaises, 1923.

Hardy, Thomas. George Meredith: a reminiscence. Cambridge: Universe Press, 1927. Twelve copies printed.

Hill, Christopher. Puritanism and Revolution: The English Revolution of the Seventeenth Century. New York: Schocken, 1958.

Hudson, Richard B. "The Meaning of Egoism in George Meredith's The Egoist." NCF, 3 (1948(, 163-176.

Kelvin, Norman. A Troubled Eden: Nature and Society in the Works of George Meredith. Standford: Standford University Press, 1961.

Lessing, Doris. "On the Golden Notebook." Partisan Review 40 (1973), 14-30.

Lindsay, Jack. George Meredith: His Life and Work. London: Bodley Head, 1956.

Mayo, Robert D. "The Egoist and The Willow Pattern." ELH, 9 (1942), 71-78.

Millet, Kate. Sexual Politics. New York: Doubleday, 1970.

Morris, John W. "Inherent Principles of Order in Richard Feverel." PMLA, 78 (1963), 333-40.

Mueller, William R. "Theological Dualism and the 'System' in Richard Feverel," ELH, 18 (1951) 138-54.

Norton, Caroline Sheridan. *English Laws for Women in the Nineteenth Century*. London: Printed for private circulation, 1854.

_____. *A letter to The Queen on the Lord Chancellor Cranworth's Marriage and Divorce Bill*. London: Longman, 1855.

_____. *Lost and Saved*. London: Hurst and Blackett, 1863.

_____. *The Wife and Woman's Reward*. 2 Vols. New York: Harper & Brothers, 1835.

O'Malley, I.B. *Women in Subjection*. London: Camelot, 1933.

Osborne, Charles C. ed. *Letters of Charles Dickens to the Baroness Burdett-Coutts*. London: John Murray, 1931.

Peel, Robert. *The Creed of Victorian Pagan*. Cambridge, Mass: Harvard University Press, 1931.

Perkins, Jane Gray. *The Life of Honourable Mrs. Norton*. New York: Henry Holt and Company, 1909.

Priestley, J.B. *George Meredith*. New York: Macmillan, 1926.

Pritchett, Victor Sawdon. *George Meredith and English Comedy*. New York: Random House, 1969.

Ratchford, Fanny E. *The Brontes' Web of Childhood*. New York: Columbia University Press, 1941.

Richardson, Samuel. *Familiar Letters on the Most Important Occasions in Common Life*. 1741, rpt. New York: Dodd, Mead, 1928.

Sassoon, Siegfried. *Meredith*. New York: Viking, 1948.

Stevenson, Lionel. *The Ordeal of George Meredith: A Biography*. New York: Scribner's, 1953.

Stevenson, Lionel., ed. *Victorian Fiction: A Guide to Research*. Cambridge: Harvard University Press, 1964.

Stone, Donald David. *Novelists in a Changing World: Meredith, James and the Transformation of English Fiction in the 1880's*. Cambridge: Harvard University Press, 1972.

Tickner, Frederick Windham. *Women in English Economic History.* London: Dent, 1923.

Tunney, Charley Dewey. "'Rose Pink and Dirty Drab'; George Meredith as a Critic." *Sewanee Review,* 39 (1931), 407-418.

Utter, R.P. and Needham, G.B. *Pamela's Daughters.* New York: Macmillan, 1936.

Van Ghent, Dorothy. "On Clarissa Harlowe." *The English Novel: Form and Function.* 1953; rpt. New York: Harper Torchbooks, 1961.

Von Racowitza, Helene (von Donniges). *Meine Beziehungen zu Ferdinand Lassalle.* Breslau: Drud und Derlag von S. Schottlaender, 1879

Von Racowitza, Helene. *Princess Helene von Racowitza: An Autobiography.* New York: Macmillan, 1911.

Wades, Alan., ed. *The Letters of W.B. Yeats.* London: Rupert Hart-Davs, 1954.

Watt, Ian. *The Rise of the Novel.* Berkeley: University of California Press, 1967.

Williams, I.M. "The Organic Structure of *The Ordeal of Richard Feverel.* RES, 18 (1967), 16-29.

Williams, Ioan., ed. *Meredith: The Critical Heritage.* London: Routledge and Kegan Paul, 1971.

Wollstonecraft, Mary. *A Vindication of the Rights of Women.* London: J. Johnson, 1792.

Woods, Alice. *George Meredith as Champion of Women and of Progressive Education.* Oxford: B. Blackwell, 1937.

Woolf, Virginia. "The Novels of George Meredith." *The Second Common Reader.* 1932; rpt. New York: Harcourt, Brace, & World, 1960, pp. 206-213.

Woolf, Virginia. *A Room of One's Own.* London: Hogarth Press, 1929.

Wright, Walter F. *Art and Substance in George Meredith.* Lincoln: University of Nebraska Press, 1953.

For Product Safety Concerns and Information please contact our EU
representative GPSR@taylorandfrancis.com
Taylor & Francis Verlag GmbH, Kaufingerstraße 24, 80331 München, Germany

www.ingramcontent.com/pod-product-compliance
Lightning Source LLC
Chambersburg PA
CBHW070402240426
43661CB00056B/2504